ACHIEVING YOUR FINANCIAL BREAKTHROUGH

A PRACTICAL GUIDE TO FINANCIAL INVESTING
PRINCIPLES, ACTING INTELLIGENTLY WITH THAT
KNOWLEDGE, AND TEACHING THE NEXT
GENERATION FOR SUSTAINED SUCCESS

DARIAN HALL

CONTENTS

Introduction   v

1. HOW MUCH SHOULD YOU INVEST   1
   Set Goals   3
   Invest What You Can   4
   The Importance of a Budget   5
   The Debt Avalanche Method   6
   The Debt Snowball Method   7
   Track Your Spending   8
   Discipline Yourself to Invest   10
   Chapter Summary   10

2. GETTING READY TO BEGIN INVESTING   13
   Start an Emergency Fund   15
   Work Toward Investing $150 Monthly   16
   Pay Yourself First   16
   Chapter Summary   17

3. HOW TO KNOW WHICH ASSETS TO BUY   19
   Common Stock   20
   Preference Stocks   22
   Growth Stock   23
   Value Stocks   24
   Seven Major Criteria You Should Consider Before Buying a   26
   Company's Stock
   The Core-Satellite Investment Strategy   29
   Chapter Summary   30

4. WHERE TO BUY ASSETS   33
   Full-Service Broker   34
   Discount Broker   35
   Margin Account   36
   Cash Accounts   36
   Chapter Summary   47

5. STARTING A PORTFOLIO 49
Primary Components of a Diversified Portfolio 51
Secondary Components of a Diversified Portfolio 53
Robo-Advisors 55
Chapter Summary 56

6. HOW MANY ASSETS SHOULD YOU OWN 59
Unsystematic Risk 60
Systematic Risk 60
Index Funds 61
Exchange-Traded Funds 62
Mutual Funds 64
Modern Portfolio Theory 68
Rebalancing Your Portfolio 69
Who Needs To Rebalance? 70
Why Do You Need To Rebalance? 71
Chapter Summary 71

7. HOW TO KNOW WHEN TO SELL YOUR STOCKS 73
Reasons To Sell Stock 74
Reasons Not To Sell a Stock 77
Common Mistakes Selling Stocks 77
When To Hold Your Stocks 79
Chapter Summary 80

8. COMPOUNDING 81
Factors That Affect Your Gains When Compounding 82
Common Compounding Mistakes To Avoid 86
Chapter Summary 88

Final Words 89
Thank You 95
References 97

INTRODUCTION

Money is a type of power, but financial education is far more impactful. Only those that understand how it works can gain control over it and increase their wealth. Unfortunately, as we went through school, most of us were never taught how to make money work for us. Instead, most of us learned how to live to work rather than how to work to live.

Investing is the most reliable way for us to take control of our financial futures. It involves investing money, time, and effort into the stock market to increase the value of the money you've invested. Investing is a tool not meant only for the rich to profit from, but also for the everyday person. It is a tool that, when used, will benefit you today and in your future.

In the following chapters, I'll walk you through a step-by-step plan for achieving your financial breakthrough. My goal is to identify the most important of these financial lessons, then associate them in a way you can find actionable. As I explain how to take responsibility for your finances and change your life in an easy-to-understand and practical manner, hopefully, you will see that with discipline and perseverance, you will be able to achieve your goals as well.

This book is designed to give anyone the knowledge and confidence in dealing with the stock market and introduce anyone to begin investing on their own to build wealth. Here are some of the things you will learn in this book:

How Much Should You Invest (Chapter 1)—You'll learn why investing in stocks is one of the best ways to grow your wealth. You will also learn how much of your income to invest, as well as the importance of setting goals, discipline, and budgeting in your overall financial situation.

Getting Ready To Begin Investing (Chapter 2)—Here, you will learn the various ways you can get your finances in order as you prepare yourself for your investment journey. You will learn what an emergency fund is and how to set one up. You will also learn the importance of having a monthly investment goal as well as the need to pay yourself first before allocating resources to fulfill your various other financial obligations.

How to Know Which Stock To Buy (Chapter 3)—You'll learn about the various kinds of stock available. You will learn the importance of researching a company before investing in its stock. You'll learn how to evaluate the stability of a company's stock by extensively researching the trends in the company's growth, its strength relative to its peers, its debt to equity ratio, its price-earning ratio, its dividend policy, leadership, and long-term strength and stability. You'll also learn about the core investment strategy and how it can stabilize your investment portfolio.

Where To Buy Assets (Chapter 4)—You'll learn about where to buy your stocks to begin investing. You will learn about the types of brokers as well as types of brokerage accounts. You will learn all the areas you should research before selecting a broker, such as the fund type, the cost, account minimums, and the available features or resources. You will also learn about some recommended brokers for beginners.

Starting A Portfolio (Chapter 5)—It's time to put all the knowledge you've acquired and research you've done into action and create your account on the platform you've chosen. You will learn the importance of diversifying your portfolio and the primary and secondary components of a well-diversified portfolio. You will learn how to diversify your assets to reduce their volatility. You will also learn about Robo Advisors, how they work, and determine if one would work best for your specific financial situation.

How Many Assets Should You Own (Chapter 6)—The appropriate number of stocks for your portfolio depends on several factors, which we'll explore in this chapter. You'll learn about investing in index funds, ETFs, mutual funds, and the other subcategories of funds under these. You will also learn about the importance of portfolio rebalancing.

How To Know When To Sell Your Stock (Chapter 7)—Your ability to make money in the stock market depends on two critical decisions: buying assets at the right time, and then selling those assets at the right time. You will learn how to determine the best time to sell your stock to maximize your investment earnings. You will learn about some good reasons to sell, the common mistakes to avoid when selling, and when to hold your stock.

Compounding (Chapter 8)—Compounding is the process of generating earnings from prior earnings. You'll learn if you should reinvest your dividends or if you should ever sell any of your dividend stocks. You'll learn the factors that affect your returns when compounding, the best compounding tips, and all the common mistakes you should avoid when compounding your assets.

We interact with money in a variety of ways, however, the purpose of this book is to teach you how to interact with money in a more beneficial way. It will assist you in nurturing the essential financial principles already recognized by many and practiced by successful people all around the world. These pages will summarize the same motivation for bigger bank accounts, greater financial triumphs, and for finding solutions to any personal financial issues you might be tackling currently. Year after year, you can rely on its principles.

The financial advice you're about to read has been shown to work. Each chapter contains new information that will help you stay in charge of your finances and gain a head start on the road to financial success. If you follow the steps outlined in this book, I guarantee that you will be able to invest wisely and incur its lasting benefits for the rest of your life. The details and applications of principles in this book will guide and provide you with the fresh perspective you need.

1

HOW MUCH SHOULD YOU INVEST

Over 2,000 years ago, a young Jewish man shared a parable with his followers of such quality that we can apply its morals for spiritual and economic gains to this day. You might know this story better as the Parable of the Talents. As the story goes, a wealthy man set to embark on a journey to a distant land decided to put his workers to a test. So before he left on this trip, he summoned three of his servants and entrusted each with a different sum of money, denominated by talents. For a little more context here, talents are monetary units valued at approximately 6,000 drachmas or equivalent to twenty years of wages.

The rich man in this story gave the first servant five talents. The second received two talents, and to the third, he gave one talent. Each was given talents according to their ability. When he returned, he summoned them to account for the talents they had received. The first and second workers invested their talents, doubled their money, and received the master's praise. However, the third servant, who was given one talent, buried his money, doing nothing to increase it. As the story goes, the master rebuked this last servant for his laziness and inactivity. This story is one of the most recognizable and commonly quoted parables in today's financial sector because it smartly illustrates the importance of investing or cultivating your talents.

Most people start saving in banks because they believe they can offer them the security to manage their money. While saving your money is essential, it is only part of the whole story. To complete your narrative, you need to put your money to work to build wealth. In other words, you would need to invest at some point. *Investing* is any strategy that enables you to control your financial security by reallocating funds into a venture to earn income or generate profit. It involves putting money, time, and effort into making a profit or getting an advantage, now or in the future.

Investing is a tool meant for anyone in any financial situation to use to build wealth. But, it is a tool that, when used wisely, will benefit you financially today and in your future. The day comes for us not to work to provide for ourselves and our families, as we once did. When that day comes, the people who would gracefully transition to a more relaxed and comfortable life would be those who have learned over time how to make their money work for them.

Ask anyone why they don't invest, and they'll likely tell you they don't have enough money to take the plunge. If they are truthful, they might confess they're too afraid to join the investing world. This is hardly surprising because investing can be scary. Your success here depends on how well your investments are doing and how much they're worth when you sell them.

The natural consequence is that even though many people know that investing is important, they are too scared to get started. Fear is the real culprit, keeping people outside the investment world and away from reaching their long-term financial goals. Instead of investing, people prefer to tuck away their money in their savings accounts because it is a more comforting idea. A more practical approach would be to set goals for yourself, have a budget, invest what you can, and be disciplined through it all.

Set Goals

The first step in achieving your financial breakthrough through investments is setting goals for the short, intermediate, and long term. Setting a budget, lowering debt, and building an emergency fund are all critical short-term goals. Long-term goals should be focused on retirement, while intermediate goals should incorporate crucial insurance plans.

Setting your financial goals is a crucial step toward financial stability. You're more inclined to spend more than you should if you're not working toward a defined goal. When you need money for unforeseen obligations, not to mention when you want to retire, you'll be short on cash. You may become trapped in a vicious cycle of credit card debt, believing that you will never have enough money to adequately insure yourself, leaving you more susceptible than necessary to deal with some of life's hazards.

No matter how much money you make, the amount you invest each year should be based on your financial goals. Unfortunately, we are currently living through a pandemic, and as such, you might feel this is not a good time to talk about investing. Possibly, you are concerned with your current working situation or focusing on several other areas of your life that take up much of your time and energy. Or it could be that the conversation about investing makes you uncomfortable. But when is there ever a good time to talk about investing?

Here's the thing: putting it off may end up costing you more than you think. According to experts, 40 percent of people have lost money as a result of procrastination. You could be losing out on some very lucrative financial rewards if you wait to invest. In fact, the time you begin investing may have a more significant impact on the amount you end up with than the amount of money you invest over time. So the sooner you put your money to work, the better off you'll be in the long run.

Also, it is not realistic to expect to foresee every calamity before it happens, but setting your investment goals will allow you to sort through potential scenarios and do your best to prepare for them. This should be a continuous process so that you can adapt your life and ambitions to the inevitable changes. Life will always throw us some curves when we least expect it. Ultimately, it would help if you are disciplined enough to continuously save the cash you earn and then eventually take steps to master how best to make your money grow. It is as simple as that.

Invest What You Can

Investing as much as you can each month is essential if you want your money to work for you. It is the best means through which you can take control of your financial situation. It allows you to build money while also providing an alternative income source in case you need it before retiring. When you invest what you can each month, you give your dollars a "task" to do: grow your wealth over time. The effects of your investment, no matter how little, will grow over time to help you achieve financial freedom. Investing improperly or not at all can result in a longer working life. When you take investing seriously, the profits you earn can help you maintain financial stability in the future. You work hard for your money, and it should return the favor. It is your responsibility to put your money to work.

Most financial planners advise investing between 10 and 15 percent of your annual income. For example, if you earn $48.000 a year, an investment goal of $400 each month will amount to 10 percent of your income, an appropriate sum for your income level. Assuming your income increases by an average of 4 percent per year, this automatically increases your investing amount by 4 percent each year as well. Within the next ten years, your annual investment sum, which started as $4,800 per year, would have grown to about $7,105. If you keep this up, and assuming you are younger now, by the time you are fifty-five, your returns would have doubled a few times over. Similarly, if you earn $35,000 a year with an investment goal of $350 a month, assuming your income increases by 4 percent over the next ten years, the value of your yearly investments, which started at $3,500 a year, would have increased to some $5,385 or more.

Another simple way to invest what you can is through your employer's retirement plan. Most workplaces provide a 401(k) or another retirement savings plan, which allows you to set aside a percentage of your paycheck and invest it for your future. Again, it's usually relatively simple to get started, and your human resources department can assist you. And here's another significant benefit of contributing to your employer's retirement plan: many companies offer an employer match, which means they'll contribute a certain amount to your retirement account based on how much you give. Plus, workplace retirement plans can come with a slew of tax benefits.

A spending plan can help you achieve your financial goals by making it easier to determine your cash flow. Like one's budget, a personal spending plan helps outline where income is earned and where expenses are incurred. However, a personal spending plan differs from a typical budget in that it is more personalized and adaptable. While many people are aware of their sources of income, such as a job wage, fewer are aware of the patterns connected with how that money is spent. You could incorporate a household spending plan, for instance, to keep track of what each member of your family spends so that you can identify strategies to save, budget, and invest what you can.

The Importance of a Budget

A common mistake most of us make when figuring out how much to save for investment is planning our savings around what we spend each month. We tend to save what we have left after spending rather than spending what is left after saving. This approach will inevitably frustrate our budding savings habit because sooner or later, it would mean no money is available for us to save for investing, mainly when expenses run high in, say, a particular month. The best way to avoid this hurdle is to reverse the destructive habit by plotting our monthly expenses around our savings goals. It's essential to have a budget to determine this efficiently.

A budget is a spending plan for your money. It estimates revenue and expenses over a specified future period and should be re-evaluated periodically. Your budget, like your personal spending plan, assists in determining where money is received and where expenses are incurred. When used in conjunction with a financial goals worksheet, one can use a reasonable budget to construct a roadmap for tracking expenditures and determining the best ways to save.

Krys was nearly $20,000 in debt, and the balance just kept growing. Finally, with no help in sight, she decided to take responsibility for her financial situation and start a budget. She made a list of eight goals she set out to complete. Those goals included getting off the credit card float, starting a regular contribution to sinking funds for general expenses, building a $1,000 emergency fund, and paying off her credit card debt, car loan, and home equity line. After her first month of serious budgeting, she saved $1,500 and crossed off the first three items on her list. By month two, she had paid $3,000. After a year of budgeting (and mind you, the year was 2020 when the world was held under siege by the COVID pandemic), she had saved over $18,000 in cash, paid off over half her debt balance, and crossed off seven of her eight initial goals.

Two ways a budget can initiate responsibility for your finances:

1. It pinpoints any debt and how much is being paid monthly for those debt(s).
2. It allows you to track your spending to determine your monthly expenses.

Pinpointing debt allows you to come up with a plan on how you will tackle it. While there are multiple methods to tackle the debt, the starting point is getting a handle on your expenses and income. Once those numbers are established, determine how best to divvy up excess income and the debt elimination path you choose. Two of the more prominent tactics are the *debt avalanche method* and the *debt snowball method*. Though, as long as you stick with it, any way you choose to pay your debt should be fine. Find the plan that works best for you.

The Debt Avalanche Method

The debt avalanche strategy entails paying as much as possible toward your highest-interest debt while making minimum payments on the remainder of your debt until it is all paid off. If you're struggling with high-interest debt, this could be an excellent way to get out of it. It focuses on paying the debt with the highest interest rate first. Then, once paid, move to the next highest, and so on until everything is paid off.

Assume you have four debts to pay off: two credit cards, a college loan, and a car loan. After you've taken care of your essential expenses and padded your emergency fund, imagine you have $650 per month left in your budget to put toward debt reduction. Using the debt avalanche technique, you will put your balances in order of highest interest rate to the lowest interest rate.

For the first credit card debt of $4,200 (22.24 percent APR), $120 is the minimum payment. The second credit card debt of $1,300 (15.74 percent APR) should have $35 as the minimum payment. A car loan of $10,750 (7.2 percent APR) has $175 as the minimum payment. The student loan of $6,400 (6.3 percent APR) should have $100 as the minimum payment and $220 as the additional payment.

Under the debt avalanche method, you would go on to make the minimum payments on each of the three loans with lower interest rates and apply your remaining funds to the $4,200 balance with the highest interest rate. According to the Bankrate credit card payoff calculator, it might take up to 15 months to pay off the first sum using the avalanche method . After you've paid off that credit card bill, you'll concentrate on the card with the next-highest interest rate. Budget the same amount ($650) per month until the debt is paid off for the best outcomes.

The Debt Snowball Method

This is a debt-reduction technique in which you pay off debt from smallest to largest, generating momentum as you finish each balance. You roll the minimum payment you were making on the smallest debt onto the next smallest debt payment when the smallest obligation for the first debt is paid in full. Under this method, you can keep paying the minimums on any debt you have, but the smallest debt gets any extra payment you can make towards that debt. After each small debt is paid, you focus that money on the next smallest debt until it is paid, and so on until everything is paid off.

Using the same budget and examples as before, you should pay off your debts in order of lowest to largest balance, independent of interest rate: Credit card debt of $1,300 (15.74 percent APR) has a minimum payment of $35. For the credit card debt of $4,200 (22.24 percent APR), $120 is the minimum payment. Student loan of $6,400 (6.3 percent APR) has a $100 minimum payment. And the car loan of $10,750 (7.2 percent APR) has a minimum payment of $175.

You'd make the minimum payments on the three other loans, then apply the remaining funds to the $1,300 debt.

Track Your Spending

Tracking your monthly spending lets you know how your income is spent and where it's being spent monthly. Every dollar counts, and accounting for them clarifies any adjustments that need to be made to save money in a particular area. Clarity on finance specifics can make it much easier to maintain the budget as you see the money's exact use, and the goals set can seem achievable by staying disciplined.

Budgeting doesn't have to be a complicated process. The 50/30/20 rule is a practical, simple method you can implement to help plan how to start or even adjust a budget to try it.

50%

This amount is dedicated to "needs," or living expenses. This can include rent or mortgage, utilities, groceries, transportation, minimum debt payments, and so on. This category should not include anything other than "needs," or expenses that have to be paid to live. Half your after-tax income should be enough to cover all your needs. If it's not, you need to consider cutting down your "wants" spending or downsizing your lifestyle to afford it within that half after-tax amount.

30%

This amount is dedicated to "wants." This can include dinner and movies, vacations, phones, shopping, and so on. It also covers upgrading selections such as choosing a more expensive steak over a cheaper hamburger, purchasing a Mercedes over a more affordable Honda, or deciding whether to watch free television via an antenna or pay for cable television. This category is generally looked at as optional expenses and consists of those little extras that we spend on to make life more pleasant. For example, instead of going to the gym, you can work out at home, cook instead of eating out, and watch sports on TV instead of purchasing tickets to the game. So, if you lack in your "needs" income, then you should look to trim down any "wants" expenses.

20%

This amount is dedicated to savings and investments. This can include saving for an emergency fund, IRA contributions, and investing in the stock market. An emergency fund should have priority while saving until you reach your emergency fund goal. After that, retirement accounts should come next, and lastly, investment accounts.

For example, with a $3,400 monthly income, you'd reserve no more than $680 for savings and debt repayment, $1,700 for needs, and $1,020 for wants. It's easy to arrange automatic transfers from your checking account to your savings account today, and for this reason, automation might be one of the simplest ways to pay yourself first each month. Figure out what's left after taking care of your necessities each month, and realign your priorities to determine what can be reasonably invested. If you find yourself coming up short, that's okay. All you need to do is look for practical ways to scale back to meet your investment goals. Explore other ways to supplement your income with side jobs if necessary.

Discipline Yourself to Invest

It's no use to make a plan here if you lack the discipline to stick to it with regular contributions. More often than we realize, we make purchases based on our emotions and the need to keep up with trends. This is further complicated because we live in an age where we can purchase whatever we want, whenever we want. These factors cause more of our hard-earned cash to slip easily through our fingers.

Start by setting aside 10 percent of your income each month. If that's too much, then test 5 percent, but do the most you can. As you pay down any debts due to your budgeting plan or any extra money you can bring in due to side jobs you have taken up, use that extra money to increase what you are setting aside each month. You can add more if you feel it's necessary. Your discipline creates your habits, your habits make your routines, and your routines are the details that make you who you are. If you genuinely want things to change in your life, developing the self-discipline to enact a plan and consistently following through is invaluable. The best way to cultivate this sense of discipline is by setting small goals for yourself and achieving them.

Chapter Summary

- Saving money is essential, but it is only part of the whole story. To complete your narrative, you need to put your money to work to build your wealth.
- The real reason most of us fail to invest all through our lives is our fear of incurring a loss.
- A budget is a spending plan for your money. It estimates revenue and expenses over a specified future period and should be re-evaluated periodically. Your budget, like your personal spending plan, assists in determining where money is received and where expenses are incurred.
- Budgeting can help you figure out how much to invest, and an even simpler way is using the 50/30/20 approach. This method allocates

20 percent of your monthly income to savings and debt repayment, 50 percent to necessities, and 30 percent to wants.

- Your discipline creates your habits, your habits make your routines, and your routines are the details that make you who you are. If you genuinely want things to change, you need the self-discipline to stop the unnecessary money drain.

In this chapter, you learned about how much you should invest as well as the importance of goal setting, discipline and budgeting in your overall financial situation. In the next chapter, you will learn how to get ready to begin investing, the importance of having an emergency fund and why you should pay yourself first.

2

GETTING READY TO BEGIN INVESTING

There's an old story I heard years ago about the importance of being prepared to achieve our goals, whatever they may be. According to this story, a middle-aged man—let's call him Saul—desirous of climbing Mount Everest, packed up his climbing gear and headed off to achieve his lifelong dream. One day, he got to a reservation at the foot of the mountain where his would-be guide greeted him. His guide checked his gear, commended his efforts to pursue his dreams, and told him to wait a while to find a good company match for the climb.

As the story goes, Saul found the latter instruction disturbing, particularly as right in front of him stood a small group of excited people, clearly set to begin their climb. So what does he do? What most of us do when we get to the threshold of our dreams and find that we might need to wait a little longer. Saul insisted on climbing with the company before him and refused to be dissuaded despite his guide's best efforts. Eventually, the guide included him in the team, gave their lines a final firm tug, and set them on their way.

Ecstatic and proud of himself for sticking to his guns, Saul took the lead as the company climbed, taking giant enthusiastic steps toward his dreams. Unfortunately, his story hit a snag, as it was bound to, because just as soon as Everest's fog engulfed the company, a large mountain lion appeared. Being out front and with significant distance between him and the rest of his company, Saul was in its direct line of attack. What can he do but call his team for help? He jumped and waved and screamed for help as loudly as the air up there could permit, but it soon became clear to Saul, who understood only English, that his teammates were all Chinese and could not imagine the reason for his frantic screams. That mountain lion eventually ate him, and the moral of the story is: *don't underestimate the importance of being ready before you climb your mountain.*

Being ready isn't about racing against time to see how fast you can get it all done. It's far more essential to focus on doing things right by learning how to pace yourself. Sometimes, this might mean going over a few areas repeatedly, so try not to be fazed. Taking the time to prepare means that you need to smooth out the rough edges before getting started on your goals.

For our context here, the best thing you can do before investing your money in any venture is to ensure that your finances are in order. Having your finances in order before you start investing will motivate you not to stop and to persevere if issues arise. Even if it's not so, that shouldn't stop you from starting—it's just the wisest course of action to take before you start. Twenty-five percent of Americans say they worry about money all the time, and studies show that two-thirds of Americans would struggle to find $1,000 to cover a financial crisis. You want to avoid being in situations like this, and for this reason, you should strive to get your finances in order.

According to a 2015 NerdWallet survey, one in four consumers shared they were sometimes surprised by how much they spent. Unfortunately, the savings rates of Americans have been falling steadily since 1975, from 17 percent to a miserly 8 percent by the end of 2019. The good news is that since you are here, you want your situation to change for the better. You are on the right path, because a shaky financial situation only leaves you in constant danger that an emergency, job loss, or health problem will disrupt your life, hurt your family, or both.

Start an Emergency Fund

It's generally a good idea to make sure we have some savings in case of an emergency, but what exactly is an emergency fund? Well, an *emergency fund* is your financial safety net for any unforeseen future mishaps and unexpected expenses. Your emergency fund exists to improve your financial security and reduce your need to draw from high-interest debt options, such as credit cards or unsecured loans.

Kesi Irvin was living an unconventional, nomadic life. She traveled the world with ease and made money by working as a hostess for top-notch travel companies. That is until her industry came to a standstill thanks to the COVID-19 pandemic. She was forced to slow down and search for a new way to earn an income, so she started a travel blog called "Kesi To and Fro." But first, Kelsi had to settle down and rent an apartment in Budapest for ten months.

She relayed that her most important lesson from all this is creating a fund to dip into when necessary. It is vital to have enough money saved to live off for six months, just in case something happens. The COVID-19 pandemic reinforced this principle for Kesi, but fortunately, you can learn from her experience and pay it forward in your own life.

A good emergency fund should typically have a minimum of three to six months' worth of expenses. An eight-month or a longer emergency fund is ideal because that's generally the length of time it takes the average person to find a job. No matter how much you make monthly, supplying your emergency fund should take precedence. Here are two simple ways to do so even if you don't bring in much money monthly:

- By setting aside 2 percent of your net income: If your net income is $35,000, this means that you can start by setting aside $700 for your emergency fund. This amount is a modest safety net to begin with, but you can slowly build on this over time.

- By saving all your tax refunds, consider diverting half or all of it into your emergency fund if you are getting any tax refund. This way, you can prepare for unforeseen situations throughout the year while simultaneously working toward your long-term financial goals.

If you don't have an emergency fund, then seriously consider starting one as soon as possible. However, please ensure it's continuously funded to maintain at least 3–6 months of your expenses if you already have one.

Work Toward Investing $150 Monthly

An excellent general rule of thumb would be to invest $150 a month initially when starting on your investing journey. As your financial situation improves over time, you can then increment that amount by whatever is feasible for you to do monthly. The monthly income for a full-time minimum-wage job in the United States is $1,255, so $150 isn't particularly an unbearable amount to invest. However, if this amount isn't practical, invest what you can comfortably. As your financial situation approves over time, gradually increase it until you reach an amount you are comfortable giving.

If you do the math and find that you cannot set $150 aside each month, take a closer look at your budget and income streams. Then, take some time and go through your expenses with a fine-tooth comb to see where you may be able to pull some extra dollars from to get to that $150 investment goal. This is where you want to look at your "wants" expenses to find some extra money and then consider your "needs" expenses if more is needed. Again, Google is an excellent tool for researching cost shortcuts you can make in your life to put a few dollars back in your pocket.

Pay Yourself First

Getting ready for your investment journey doesn't mean a life of frugality where you say no to everything. On the contrary, you can have a great time living your life while simultaneously saving money. Balancing your financial needs against your daily emotional needs means that while you keep your financial house in order, you are also organized enough to enjoy life to the fullest.

In a recent study, over 1,000 students graduating from the University of British Columbia completed a survey set up to determine whether they tend to value time over money or vice versa. Some of the students reported prioritizing time, while the rest placed more value on money. Less than a year after graduation, the researchers found that the students who prioritized money ended up less happy than their classmates who prioritize their time.

A novel concept is known to many but practiced by few is paying yourself first. Paying yourself involves setting aside money into savings or retirement accounts before paying any bills or obligations. This can be done manually or even automated, as most financial institutions offer direct deposits. The most challenging aspect of accepting this has always been the mental switch that has to be turned on to view this concept positively. Society influences us to want to buy, and not only that, to buy for selfish reasons to satiate the gratification now mentality being pushed on us. Paying yourself first encourages sound fiscal habits, and setting aside the money beforehand removes the rationalizations we make on how we will spend it. Be practical and disciplined, and you will begin to see positive results once you start living this way.

Chapter Summary

- The emergency fund is your financial safety net and should be the first item you work on preparing to invest. A recommended amount would be three to six months of expenses, and if that may be too much for you, try saving 2 percent of your net income or use tax refunds to fund the account.
- The $150 a month investing goal is a good benchmark to start with. As your budget and finances change over time, you should be able to increase this amount steadily. If $150 is a stretch, start

with as much as you can spare but continue to build up the
amount.
- Paying yourself first involves setting income aside before paying
  any other obligations. Developing this habit grows sound fiscal
  habits with how you interact with money.

In this chapter, you learned how to get ready to begin investing. You also
learned the importance of an emergency fund, having a monthly investment goal, and paying yourself first. In the next chapter you will learn
about the types of stock, how to know which stocks to buy, what to research
before you buy a company's stock, and the core-satellite investment
strategy.

3

HOW TO KNOW WHICH ASSETS TO BUY

A little boy walks into a toy store with his dad and when asked what toy he loved the most, was confused by the different sorts on display before him. "What do I choose? What do I choose? Do I pick a car, a comic book, or some new legos?" He asked himself. "Come on, kid, we don't have all day," his dad says, looking at his wristwatch and gradually getting irked by his son's indecision. "I love these. No wait, these are awesome too," replies the boy, strolling down the aisles, picking up toys and putting them back. He couldn't make up his mind.

"Ben, you need to make up your mind," says his father, "my break time is almost over, and I have to get back to the office." Panicking in the way only kids do, the boy runs around the store, his eyes moving from one shelf to another. Every new toy looked better than the last, but try as he might, he could not make a decision. Eventually, his father throws his hands in the air and declares that they could always return some other day. He grabs his son by the hand, and they walk out of the store into the hot summer afternoon empty-handed, the father thinking of his next business meeting for the day, the son with tears in his eyes. The boy loved all the toys from that store but ended up with nothing because he couldn't pick even one. We're all that boy, and the world is our toy store.

Life presents us all with a myriad of options. These options often relate to various areas of our lives: career, education, relationships, investments, and other vital issues. Our inability to choose well largely stems from a fear of making the wrong choice and worries of regret in the future. As our brain goes about computing all these thoughts, we fail to consider a far more significant danger: making no decision at all, going nowhere, doing nothing, and ending up empty-handed.

A *stock* (also known as *equity*) is a security that represents the ownership of a fraction of a corporation. This entitles the stock owner to a proportion of the corporation's assets and profits equal to how much stock they own. Units of stock are called *shares*. When you own shares of stock in a company, you can earn returns on your investment when your stock value appreciates and if your stocks pay dividends, as many do. A *dividend* is a sum of money paid regularly (typically quarterly) by a company to its shareholders out of its profits (or *reserves*).

There are so many stock options available for you to choose from on your investment journey, all with different benefits and associated risks. These include the following:

Common Stock

Common stock is a security that represents ownership in a company or corporation. It is reported on the stockholder's equity section of their balance sheet, and common stockholders elect its board of directors.

Pros:

- Common stock performs better than bonds, deposit certificates, and other types of investment packages. There are no limits to the amount of money you can gain when your stock value increases, and it yields higher rates of returns when held for more extended periods.
- It is a limited liability investment. When you invest in common stock, whatever amount you invested in initially would be the most

you would lose in the event of the company's liquidation. You also have legal protection against whatever legal or illegal problems arise within the company because such would fall outside the scope of your financial investment.

- You can easily buy or sell your common stock at any time. This type of stock is a very liquid investment that can be converted into cash nearly instantly. Almost any trading platform will allow you to open an account at any moment to purchase this asset.

Cons:

- Common stock prices fluctuate easily, and their value often changes with no warning. In a single day, your portfolio can lose a lot of money because stock markets all across the world are highly volatile. Price movements of several percentage points may frequently occur throughout a single trading session. Not only may your portfolio earn a significant sum in a short time, but it also has the ability to lose everything in one day.
- As a common stockholder with limited liability, your participation in the decision-making process is limited, and you will not have as much control as other stockholders would.
- Common stockholders receive whatever assets remain after creditors, bondholders, and preferred stockholders are paid if a company is liquidated.
- Professional traders and institutional investors have more time and access to sophisticated financial models to investigate companies and monitor the stock market. Beginners who buy common stocks often approach the stock market by guesswork unless they have a specific investing strategy in mind. To make a profit, you must compete with those professionals. If you don't have the same amount of time as they have, this indicates their job has a competitive advantage over your investing efforts. This can be quite daunting.

Preference Stocks

A *preference stock* is a type of stock that offers its holders a higher claim on a company's assets and earnings than common stock. This means that preferred stockholders receive regular dividends and are repaid first in the event of a bankruptcy or merger. Thus, preferred stock combines common stock and bonds in one security, including regular income and ownership.

Pros:

- Preference stockholders receive higher and regular dividends because they assume more risk than common stockholders. They also enjoy the right to receive your dividend payments before the common shareholders do.
- If the company fails, preferred stockholders are in line ahead of common stock shareholders to get back their money.
- There are potential returns from callable preference stock. *Callable preferred stock* is a type of preferred stock in which the issuing company retains the right to call in or redeem the stock at a preset price after a specified date.
- *Convertible preferred stocks* are preferred stock shares that allow the holder to convert them into a fixed number of common stock shares after a predetermined date.

Cons:

- Unlike the common stockholders, preference shareholders do not possess voting rights in the personal matters of the company. This means that its owners have no say in the corporation's major decisions, such as mergers or amendments to the corporate charter. They are also unable to vote in the annual shareholder meetings for the election of the board of directors.
- There is limited growth potential for preference stocks because the dividends paid to the preference shareholders by the issuing company are fixed. This means that any additional profits that

ought to be available to the dividends of preference shareholders can be maximized by the company with no consequences. The preferential shareholders, therefore, have no claim over the surplus returns of the company.

- Preferred stocks are often purchased for their high current dividends. They typically have fixed dividends, making them comparable to other fixed income products such as bonds. Fixed dividends make preferred shares more susceptible to interest rate changes: as interest rates rise, fixed income securities prices fall.
- Dividends on preferred stock are not guaranteed. If an issuer runs into financial difficulties, preferred stock dividends may be reduced or suspended. Preferred stock owners would then be stuck with shares with no upward potential and no dividends, which no one wants.
- Preferred shareholders have priority over regular shareholders in bringing property claims to recoup their investment if the issuer files for bankruptcy, but they lag behind bondholders. When it comes time to pay preferred shareholders, there are usually no assets remaining. As a result, preferred shareholders can suffer the same total loss as regular stockholders despite their seniority.

Growth Stock

A *growth stock* is any share in a company that generates such substantial and sustainable positive cash flow that it is anticipated to grow significantly above the average growth for the market. Most of these stocks do not pay dividends. This is because growth stock issuers are typically businesses that seek to reinvest any profits to accelerate growth in the short term. Thus, when investors buy growth stocks, they expect to profit from capital gains when they sell their shares in the future. Companies here tend to be relatively new or small and can be found in growth sectors like technology or biotech.

Pros:

- As the name suggests, growth stocks can appreciate significantly in the long term and yield impressive returns. Even when the economy is declining, more earnings growth may be feasible.
- Opportunity to invest in emerging assets or businesses. You have the chance to be a part of something amazing if you concentrate on emerging growth investments.
- It can help you compound your wealth. When you reinvest your capital gains from a growth stock, this can produce a compounding effect.

Cons:

- A significant disadvantage of a growth stock is its high risk factor. This is because a growth stock can be highly volatile—most shares in the stock market trade in cycles. If investors acquire growth stocks when the market shifts its focus elsewhere, they may underperform for years.
- To fully benefit from a growth stock, you need to be willing to hold the stock for at least five to ten years. This means that if your financial goal is to create fast profit within a short time frame, growth stock would be unwise for you.
- Growth stocks are mostly new companies, and because they are young, these companies rarely pay out dividends in their early stages. It's possible that you won't get any dividends. Many growth firms reinvest their earnings in the company rather than issuing dividends to their shareholders. This can lead to higher future appreciation, but it also means that investors only profit from the sale of the shares rather than through dividend payments. If you sell too soon, you'll miss out on future gains. If you sell too late, your earnings will dwindle, and you will lose money.

Value Stocks

A *value stock* is a share of a corporation that appears to trade at a lower price relative to its fundamentals, such as dividends, earnings, or sales. A value stock typically has a lower equity price than other companies in the same industry. Value stocks can also be found in a sector that trades at a lower price than the overall market. Therefore, they are considered under-valued in the financial market because their prices remain low regardless of their seemingly strong performance.

Pros:

- Value stock can fetch good returns. This is possible because, as an investor, you can buy value stock at lower prices and sell above their perceived value.
- There are lower risks associated with value stock, and they are generally stable.
- Most value stocks pay reasonable sums of money to their holders as dividends because they recognize the need to make their stocks attractive to investors.
- Value stockholders stand to gain massively when the financial market also recognizes that their stocks were undervalued. When this happens, the value of the stocks can increase exponentially and earn their holders' good returns.

Cons:

- Undervalued stocks worth investing in are challenging to identify. This demands experience and expertise on the part of the investor.
- As a value stockholder, you may have to hold for years while waiting for market conditions to change in your favor. Even then, your patience may still not yield high returns.
- Committing your funds to several value stocks may expose you to substantial risks because your portfolio would be poorly diversified.

Investing according to your risk profile, especially while younger, is a wise plan for beginners in investing. Your *risk profile* is your evaluation of your willingness and practical ability to take on investment risks. Your risk capacity is simply the level of investment losses that you can afford to take. While younger, there's a long time on the horizon for investing, allowing you to assume a bit more risk for better returns. If older, there's still room for risk for better returns, but it needs to be planned out more thoroughly to reduce any volatility. *Volatility* is the degree of variation of a trading price series over time. Since their prices are believed to be reasonably unpredictable, volatile assets tend to be riskier than the less volatile assets. Your risk profile is important because it will help you mitigate unnecessary risks and determine what you want your investment portfolio to achieve.

Your *investment portfolio* is a compilation of all your financial assets such as closed-end funds, ETFs, equities, bond funds, stock holdings, commodities, and all cash equivalents. It's best to figure out what you want your investment portfolio to achieve for you and the timeframe to achieve that goal before you begin to invest actively. Investors generally aim for a return by mixing the securities in their portfolios in a way that reflects their risk tolerance and actualizes their financial goals. Therefore, research is your friend here, and there are seven significant criteria you should consider before buying a company's stock.

Seven Major Criteria You Should Consider Before Buying a Company's Stock

I. **Research trends in the company's growth.** Your research should analyze the company's data over a given time to demonstrate whether or not the company's earnings have increased. A company's *earnings* are its after-tax net income, which plays a massive role in determining its stock price. The prospectus can be helpful here, for looking at the company's earnings growth over some time. A *prospectus* is a formal document required by and filed with the Securities and Exchange Commission (SEC) that provides details about an investment offering to the public. A prospectus is filed for offerings of stocks, bonds, and mutual funds. The document can help investors make more informed investment decisions because it contains a host of relevant information about investment security.

· · ·

2. Research the company's strength relative to its peers. By all means, do your homework on the industry to properly assess the presence or absence of its potential for future growth. In doing so, compare the company to peers within its industry and review its performance over the same period. Peer comparison assumes that the peer group is, on average, reasonably valued. This will help you determine how well the company truly fares in its industry and if buying its stock would be worth the investment.

3. Research the company's debt to equity ratio and see if it's in line with industry norms. All companies carry debt, but you can use the debt to equity ratio to evaluate a company's financial health. The *debt to equity ratio* measures the difference between ordinary shareholders' equity and creditors' shareholding in a corporation. It's a long-term solvency ratio that shows how sound a company's long-term financial practices are. A high debt-to-equity ratio can be a red flag because it shows that the company is struggling. Research the industry norms because the generally acceptable debt to equity ratios depend primarily on the industry.

4. Research the company's price-earning ratio. The *price-earning ratio* is a popular valuation indicator that measures how well a stock performs relative to its earnings. To find the price-earnings ratio, divide the company's share price by its earnings per share. It helps investors determine if a stock is valued appropriately based on its current price and earnings per share. It is based on the company's past and future earnings, and a higher price-to-earnings ratio means that the stock price is high compared to company earnings and, as such, may be overvalued. Alternatively, a low price to earnings ratio shows that the share price is low compared to company earnings and is undervalued.

5. Research the company's dividend policy if it offers one. Dividends are how companies distribute their profit, and their payment needs to be approved by the company directors before they can be paid out. The company's strategy directs the frequency with which dividends are paid out, and the amount that they pay out is referred to as its *dividend policy.*

6. Research the company leadership and their effectiveness. Without effective leadership, all other business resources will be ineffective. When you invest in a company with strong leadership, you may expect to gain a considerable competitive advantage since the company will improve its bottom line, drive strategy execution, and grow the value of your shares while the company navigates change. The leadership of a business can be the difference between a company's success or failings, so take this part of your research seriously.

7. Research the long-term strength and stability of the company. The stock market is inherently volatile, at least from day to day and year to year. Further, a company's market worth will depreciate at some point. What matters most, though, is long-term stability. Examine this closely before you buy a company's stock. It's a good bet to invest in a stable company that only appears to have significant problems when everyone else does. A stable company generally exhibits items on this list: it grows revenues, keeps debt low, is competitive in its field, and has effective leadership.

Finding the perfect stock to purchase can be very rewarding, but when should you go in and buy the shares? Knowing when to buy can be just as important as what you buy. When stocks go on sale and when stocks are undervalued are two great times to purchase shares.

Purchasing stocks on sale is also known as buying on the dip. A *dip* is usually only a temporary drop in prices in one sector, a single stock, or across a market. More severe price drops are after stock market downturns, corrections, and crashes. A *market downturn* is a period where the stock market continues to decline. Downturns can sometimes lead to recessions but not necessarily crashes or depressions.

A *market correction* is the negative movement of prices of 10 percent in a major index such as the Dow Jones Industrial Average. Markets and indexes may experience stock market corrections for days, weeks, or even longer. A *market crash* is a sudden, sharp drop in prices. The market crash in 1929, which brought upon the Great Depression in the United States, is probably the most infamous stock market crash. Stocks are generally undervalued during these market fluctuations. These downtimes make ideal moments to purchase stocks in solid, stable companies that have researched and know will bounce back with solid returns once the market gets stable.

There are several things you should never do during any of these market moments. These will be introduced now but will be further explained in upcoming chapters:

- Panic
- Sell your shares when prices fall
- Attempt to time the market
- Take on new debt
- Agree to cosign loans for others
- Ignore your investment plan

The Core-Satellite Investment Strategy

A recommended investment strategy for beginner or seasoned investors is the core-satellite strategy. By design, a *core investment strategy* is low-risk. It has the advantages of index funds—lower costs, greater diversification, tax efficiency, and reduced volatility—with the prospect of increased returns. An *index fund* is a type of mutual fund or exchange-traded fund (ETF) with a portfolio constructed to match or track the components of a financial market index, such as the Standard & Poor's Index (S&P 500). This strategy can either be set up yourself or through a financial advisor. Still, to save money on the fees associated with that, I would recommend doing it yourself, as it's not complicated to do so with some time and effort spent researching.

Core-satellite brings greater discipline and stability to an investment port-folio by:

- Reducing reliance on "picking winners" or chasing fund manager returns.
- Providing greater portfolio diversification.
- Potentially improving after-tax returns by taking maximum advantage of capital gains discounts.
- Reducing overall fund management and transaction costs.

Regardless of the specific investments, cost, portfolio volatility, and invest-ment returns are the underlying considerations of this strategy. The general rule of thumb for portfolio balancing is 80/20. Still, it can be adjusted to suit your investment risk profile, core fund type style, or even just personal preference: the 80 being 80 percent, or the core of the portfolio. In addition, investments are made up of index funds or your preferred fund type: the 20 being 20 percent, or the satellite of the portfolio. Finally, investments are made up of actively managed funds, stocks, or other direct investments that have the potential to overperform. This balancing setup gives the ideal exposure to diversification and potential returns while mitigating excessive costs and potential losses.

The core-satellite approach provides an opportunity to access the best aspects of all worlds. Stable, better than average performance, limited volatility, and cost-effectiveness combine in a flexible package designed for the average person.

Chapter Summary

- Research should be your next step before buying a stock and yours should focus on the following seven criteria: trends in the earnings and growth of the company, the company's strengths in relation to its peers, the company's debt to equity ratio, its price to earnings ratio, its dividend policy, the effectiveness of the leadership team, and long term strength and stability of the company.

- The two best times to buy are when the stock is on sale and when the stock is undervalued.
- The core-satellite investment strategy is an investment strategy in which the portfolio is divided into two parts. The first and more significant part, the core, is managed passively to minimize costs, risks, and tax liability. The second part, the satellite, is managed actively to provide your portfolio with the opportunity to outperform the stock market.

In this chapter, you learned about how to know which assets to buy, the criteria to research into before buying a company's shares, the best times to buy shares, and the core-satellite investment strategy. In the next chapter you will learn more about where to buy your stocks, types of brokers and accounts, fund types, and the best brokers for beginners.

4

WHERE TO BUY ASSETS

There's a story about a crew who were getting ready to set sail and discovered, to their dismay, that the ship's engine had failed. The ship's captain tried all he could to remedy this, but eventually, he had to cancel the sail and notify the ship's owners of the challenge. Along came the owners, who called in favors from every seaport their ship had ever docked. Professional engineers came one after another, but hours later, none of them could figure out how to fix the broken engine. Finally, just as the sun began to set, somebody recommended an old fisherman who had been repairing ships from his teenage years. He lacked the educational background of all the professional engineers who had examined the ship before him. He carried a large bag of tools with him and, when he arrived, immediately went to work.

He inspected the engine thoroughly, from top to bottom, while the desperate ship owners watched, hoping he wouldn't further damage the ship's engine. Eventually, the old man reached into his bag and pulled out a basic hammer. He gently stooped over an angle of the engine and tapped something lightly. Instantly, the ship's engine lurched into life. The old man carefully put his hammer away, picked up his tool bag, and announced that the engine was fixed! A few days later, when the ship was already out at sea, the owners received an invoice from the old man for $10,001. "What?!" the owners exclaimed. "He hardly did anything!" So they wrote to the man, "Please send us a detailed invoice." As the story goes, the old man sent an invoice that read:

Tapping with a hammer $1.00

Knowing where to tap $10,000.00

The type of investor you discover you are, and the investing features you find most important, will lead you to where to best buy your stocks. Most, if not all, investing is done online, and finding the best online broker for beginners can vary depending on your specific needs and preferences. For example, do you prefer a complex and full-featured stock trading platform, or would a simple, user-friendly app be enough?

When you want to buy stock in a company, you can't simply call up the company and buy shares, nor can you walk into your local bank and invest. Instead, you'll need a specialized type of account that can facilitate these transactions. A *stockbroker* is an entity that facilitates the buying and selling of marketable securities like stocks and exchange-traded funds (ETFs). Through a stockbroker, you can open a *brokerage account*, which is a specialized financial account that is designed to hold investments as well as cash.

There are two main types of stockbrokers: *full-service* and *discount*. The cost and level of service for each type are different and should be considered when choosing how to invest.

Full-Service Broker

- It can be considered an "old style" broker, meaning it has a physical location where an actual person, or stockbroker, takes and executes the client's buy/sell orders.
- Provides personalized investment planning services, such as advice on which stocks to buy, tax guidance, and retirement planning.

Individual stockbrokers and/or financial advisors are allocated to clients. At a full-service brokerage firm, they are the primary point of contact.

- It is generally more expensive as commissions at full-service brokerages are much higher than those at discount brokers.
- Best suited for high net worth investors that require a personal level of service for their needs. Beginners who require professional investment advice or different forms of assistance with their financial planning outside of investing can also choose full-service brokers.

Discount Broker

- A company that allows investors to buy and sell investments online.
- Discount brokers do not offer the same level of investing advice or guidance as full-service brokers.
- The process of buying/selling stocks with a discount broker is mainly user-generated.
- They're cheaper than full-service brokers, with most brokers offering $0 commission stock trading. Investors who trade regularly benefit from discount brokers' lower commissions.
- Best suited for beginner investors, mainly because of its affordability. Discount brokers are also a good choice for investors who don't require guidance, have modest holdings, or simply want their trades done.

The type of broker that will work best for you will depend on your specific situation. However, for most beginners, the low cost of getting started makes using a discount broker the best option. As discount brokers are becoming more feature-rich with educational resources, stock research, and how-to articles at no extra cost, this is the path I recommend the readers of this book take.

In addition to types of brokerages, there are two types of accounts you can hold at a brokerage, *margin accounts* and *cash accounts*.

Margin Account

- Margin accounts are brokerage accounts that let you borrow money to make a trade. The securities and cash purchased in the account serve as collateral for the loan, which has a fixed interest rate. For this reason, buying stock on margin exposes you to risks.
- When you buy shares on margin, you can boost the size of your investment by leveraging the value of assets you already hold.
- If an investor uses margin funds to purchase assets and those stocks rise in value beyond the interest rate imposed on the funds, the investor will earn a higher total return than if they had purchased securities with their own money. This is one of the benefits of employing margin funds.
- You can make profits on margin accounts by short selling. *Short selling* is a complex strategy in which an investor attempts to profit from a falling stock price. To sell securities short, you must first borrow stock from a brokerage business, which requires that you have a margin account approved. After borrowing shares, you sell them and then repurchase them at a lower price at a later period. Your profit would be the difference between the proceeds of the original sale and the cost of buying back the shares.
- You get more flexibility in building your portfolio, but any investment losses may encompass both borrowed and personal funds. A margin account loan also comes with interest.

Cash Accounts

- Unlike a margin account, a cash account is a form of brokerage account in which the investor must pay the entire purchase price for the shares. Here, you are not allowed to borrow funds from your broker to cover your account transactions.

- When buying stocks in a cash account, the investor must either deposit enough cash to cover the deal or sell other securities on the same trading day to cover the buy order.
- Your potential losses in a cash account are always limited to the amount you invest. This is a primary reason why new investors are encouraged to begin their investment journeys with cash brokerage accounts.
- A margin call will never be made on an investor's cash account if they have securities in it because there is no margin debt. Investors also avoid the risk of their investments being lost owing to *rehypothecation exposure*. This occurs when the investor's shares are used as collateral for the broker's third-party loans.

Whether you choose a discount broker or a full-service broker, the process for opening a brokerage account is similar to the process of opening a checking or savings account. Using an online broker should take about fifteen minutes and involve filling out a few simple forms. During the process, make sure to have a driver's license or some form of ID on hand, such as another state-issued ID or US passport to verify your identity. Also, have your Social Security number, which is also used to verify your identity and needed for tax purposes, and some funding method ready to use. The easiest way to fund a new brokerage account is by ACH transfer from your bank account.

Here are four factors that you should consider when choosing a brokerage account:

1. Funds Types

A regular brokerage account, also known as a taxable brokerage account or a non-retirement account, allows you to invest in various assets such as stocks, mutual funds, bonds, exchange-traded funds, and more. Individual stocks may not be suitable for everyone, so mutual funds may be an alternative. Ideally, the broker will offer a large selection of no-fee options to choose from.

. . .

2. Account Minimums

Some brokerage houses may require a minimum deposit of $1,000, $2,000, or more. Others may allow you to start an account with a lesser deposit as long as you agree to have money deposited from a connected checking or savings account regularly, usually monthly. In addition, most online brokers don't have minimum initial deposit requirements. Instead, some offer incentives such as free stocks when you fund your account with a certain amount of money.

3. Costs

As a result of adopting new market norms, exchange and clearing transaction fees can sometimes become a little complicated. New innovative fee systems are in development all the time to attract new investors. Do your research and find out if there are any hidden costs, because a request not included in the agreed scope of work may result in a fee. The good news here is that most online brokers don't have any commission, stock trade, or ETF trade fees associated with them. However, there are fees associated with most specific trades, such as broker-assisted trades, mutual fund trades, or option trading (all of which are not in the scope of this book).

4. Features/Resources

Online brokers increasingly offer more features and resources such as educational resources, third-party stock research, technology, familiarity, proprietary fund options, live news updates, articles, and more.

Here are five features/resources to look for when choosing a brokerage account:

1. Research

Most discount brokers offer a base level of research that you can use on their platform. In addition, most provide high-level information, including charts, graphs, press release information, company financial information, and more. If you're a more experienced investor, you might want more research and analytical tools. Some brokerages provide detailed analyst ratings and access to third-party research and screeners to assist you in deciding between the numerous investment possibilities available.

2. Education

Most discount brokers offer a plethora of information, including how to use their platform effectively, execute various types of trades on their platform, invest glossaries, and more. What resources does the company provide? Are there any educational articles? Do you desire guidance, and are they willing to offer it to you? Are there any webinars or other tutorials available? If you want to learn more about investing, seek a firm that offers beginner classes. If your broker provides some educational tools, use them to inform your investing choice.

3. Trading Simulators

A *stock market simulator* is a computer program or application that aims to replicate or imitate some or all aspects of a live stock market so that a participant can practice trading stocks without risking any money. Does the platform offer trading simulators? If so, use this feature to simulate live stock market features to practice trading stocks at no risk. Simulators can assist you in learning how to calculate trading costs and do stock analysis. Simulators use standard analytical methods like price/earnings ratios and other financial measures. This tool can also be used to test new or different investment strategies.

4. Customer Support

Brokers that offer highly visible customer support differentiate themselves from the rest of the pack. Bad customer support is a dead giveaway that you're dealing with a scammer. When they don't provide you with the support you need, you run the risk of being taken advantage of. Most brokers in the market guarantee that you will have access to customer support twenty-four hours a day, but it is a good idea to double-check ahead of time to ensure that you don't wind up with one that doesn't care about you. If you find a platform that goes above and beyond your expectations, that may be the tipping point for choosing them over other brokers.

5. Mobile Apps

Most discount brokers offer very capable mobile apps for their platform that provide the same functionality as their website or desktop application and are available on virtually every available platform (iOS, Android, Windows). The majority of mobile trading apps today are designed to show all of your investments and their performance in one place. You should be able to buy and sell your shares whenever you like through your app, as well as evaluate your earnings and losses.

To help facilitate your decision on which broker may work best for you, here are six current discount broker choices that I would encourage you to consider.

1. TD Ameritrade

TD Ameritrade is a broker that provides an online trading platform for financial assets. Different stock options, futures contracts, ETFs, cryptocurrencies, fixed income securities, and wealth management services are all examples of what TD Ameritrade offers. This platform provides more than enough complementary research, with educational components that range from introductory to advanced. In addition, they offer complete suites of services, account types, and investments, allowing you to do just about anything on their platform and all for $0 commission on most of their major products.

Pros:

- Offers more than 4,100 no-transaction-fee mutual funds.
- On its website, TD Ameritrade provides imitation trading accounts. Its virtual simulator, paperMoney, is a desktop-based program aimed at advanced and frequent traders. It comes with $100,000 in practice "money" and access to a margin account, making it an excellent opportunity to try out a new platform before committing to a real-money account.
- You can trade almost anything—stocks, bonds, options, forex, and more.
- Their research and education offers are top-notch, including reports from MorningStar, CFRA, and more.

Cons:

- Has more than 13,000 mutual funds where if they are not fee-free, you will pay a hefty fee for no-load funds, and even more in commission for load funds.
- Does not offer fractional purchases of stocks.

(TD Ameritrade, "Why TD Ameritrade," n.d.)

2. Fidelity

This platform has some of the best research and customer support in the industry. The Fidelity website's workflow for assessing or trading current positions is simple—you'll find links to news and analysis for tickers in your portfolio or watchlist. In addition, it's very investor-friendly, offering no account minimums, no commissions on ETF or stock trades, and you'll generally avoid extra fees on routine services provided by the company.

Pros:

- Very investor-friendly, minimizing fees charged to you for the majority of their offered services.
- Offers no-transaction-fee mutual funds and fee-free mutual funds, which offer no transaction fees, as the name suggests, for the former funds, and the latter funds have no expense ratio, both of which can save you a lot of money.
- It has a fractional share program, which allows purchasing partial shares for as little as $1.

Cons:

- While offering the basics most will need for investing—stocks, bonds, ETFs, mutual funds, and options—it provides nothing in niche sectors such as forex or futures trading.
- New account or account bonuses pale in comparison to what other brokers offer.
- Slow live chats and slower account verification.
- High mutual fund fees and margin rates.

(Fidelity, "The Fidelity Advantage: A Clear Choice," n.d.)

3. E*Trade

The E*trade website is simple to navigate and intuitive, making it an excellent resource for beginners who are nervous about investing online for the first time. This platform caters to two different groups, beginner investors and more advanced traders, each with different needs and expectations, and the broker does an adequate job serving both. With discounted options commissions, a wide selection of no-transaction-fee mutual funds, and plenty of research offerings, this platform is an excellent choice for newer investors.

Pros:

- While offering the basics most will need for investing—stocks, bonds, ETFs, mutual funds, and options—it also offers futures, a high-risk security in the market.
- Provides its daily commentary on the market and offers third-party research, articles, videos, classes, and a library of finance topics.
- Their trading platforms shine and stand out from other brokers. They offer a base platform that provides an excellent package for beginner investors and a higher level platform for more advanced users.

Cons:

- You can reinvest dividends into fractional shares, but the platform doesn't allow you to purchase partial shares.
- Charges transfer fees if you want to move your money from them to another brokerage account.
- The platform only trades in US markets, no forex.
- Slow live chat.

(E*Trade, "Why E*Trade," n.d.)

4. Vanguard

Vanguard is undoubtedly a popular name in the brokerage sector, having managed trillions of dollars on behalf of investors worldwide. It offers dozens of funds that don't charge a commission or transaction fee, allowing you to put all of your money into the fund and increase your return. Vanguard is an excellent option for fund investors and a good choice for long-term investors with low trading requirements. This platform will work just fine for individual investors who want to buy and hold their investments, especially Vanguard funds. They have many low-cost funds, giving you a ton of options to trade without commission or transaction fees.

Pros:

- Leader in low-cost funds.
- It has a ton of retirement planning tools, calculators, and resources for investors of all ages and all types.
- Vanguard offers competitive long-term performance, outstanding service, and affordable prices regardless of how much you invest.
- To trade ETFs (exchange-traded funds) and stocks online, all Vanguard clients pay no commission. You can also choose from over 160 Vanguard no-transaction-fee mutual funds and over 3,000 funds from other providers.

Cons:

- You can reinvest dividends and mutual funds into fractional shares, but it doesn't allow you to purchase partial shares.
- Basic trading platform that works for users who plan on trading only a few times a year, but it's not really for active traders.
- High minimums for mutual funds.
- Account fees and options commissions sit at the high end of the industry.

(Vanguard, "Why Investors Choose Vanguard," n.d.)

5. Webull

Webull, a mobile app-based brokerage, was created a few years ago, and it offers commission-free stock and exchange-traded fund (ETF) trading. This platform is best suited for intermediate investors, active traders, options traders, and cryptocurrency traders. With free trading, no account minimums, and even no-cost option trading, their services made Webull one of the best platforms for newcomers to experience.

Pros:

- Allows you to trade cryptocurrency directly.
- Offers instant funding on deposits up to $1,000.
- Webull has some of the lowest brokerage fees while still providing powerful trading tools for beginners.
- It offers a paper trading account, which is a cool tool that mimics an actual trading process with virtual money so you can practice various techniques or investment strategies.

Cons:

- Offers no mutual funds on its platform.
- It doesn't provide a lot of free fundamental research.
- It doesn't provide fractional shares as purchases or dividend reinvestments.

(Webull, "Enjoy Tech. Enjoy Investing," n.d.)

6. Ally Invest

Ally Invest is a self-directed online brokerage that offers automatic investing, retirement funds, and forex trading. This platform will work just fine for individual investors who want to buy and hold their investments. They have some of the best promotional incentives for new accounts. If you are already banking with them, integrating your new investment account into your banking/savings is almost too easy.

Pros:

- Banking integration makes consolidating accounts very easy and convenient.
- Excellent promotional bonuses when you create an investment account with them.

- No-fee stock and options commissions and no account minimums.
- Commission-free trades on eligible US stocks, options, and ETFs.
- The platform is easy to navigate and provides reliable trading tools for investors.

Cons:

- It doesn't offer any no-transaction-fee mutual funds.
- It has a slightly above average trading platform.
- It has no branches.

(Ally Invest, "Investing With Us," n.d.)

Chapter Summary

- A stock broker is an entity that facilitates the buying and selling of marketable securities like stocks and exchange traded funds (ETFs).
- There are two major types of stock brokers: full service brokers and discount brokers. A full-service stockbroker offers a variety of financial services to clients and these include: financial planning, business and personal home loans, banking services, and asset management. A discount broker is a company that allows investors to buy and sell investments online. They are also cheaper than full-service brokers.
- There are four factors that you should consider when choosing a brokerage account and these are: the fund type, the cost, account minimums, and the available features or resources.
- Five features/resources to look for when choosing a brokerage account include: research, education, trading simulators, customer support and the mobile app available.
- To help facilitate your decision on which broker may work best for you, the six current discount broker choices that I would encourage you to consider are: TD Ameritrade, Fidelity, E*Trade,

Vanguard, Webull, and Ally Invest. These brokers offer full suites of services, account types, and investments allowing you to do just about anything on their platform and all for little or no commission on most of their major products.

In this chapter, you learned about where to buy your stocks, types of brokers and accounts, fund types, areas to research before selecting a broker, and recommended brokers for beginners. In the next chapter you will learn how to start your investment portfolio and the types of stocks your portfolio can hold.

5

STARTING A PORTFOLIO

There's an old riddle that you might have heard. It asks if five frogs are sitting on the fence and one frog decides to jump, how many would be left? If your answer is "four," then you must have learned a thing or two from your math teacher back in the day. Unfortunately, though, the riddle is not a test of your math abilities but seeks to throw more light on a standard life problem. The correct answer is "five." Yes, all five frogs are still sitting there on that fence. Why? Because that one frog only *decided* to jump, it hasn't jumped yet. The journey starts with a single step—not by merely choosing to take that step.

It's time to put all the knowledge you've acquired and research you've done into action and create and fund your account on the platform you've chosen. This is the point in the journey where it's time to get intentional and start moving with purpose to achieve that financial breakthrough we are working to achieve. Creating your portfolio should be a smooth process as we've gone over how much you should invest, getting everything together for you to begin investing, learning how to know which stocks to buy, and learning where to buy stocks. This knowledge base we've been building over these last chapters has hopefully built your confidence to believe in all the decisions you have made thus far as the best route to take during this process.

With the initial funding of your portfolio, a good plan of action would be to spread that funding over all the investments you plan on funding, at least initially. When starting your portfolio, focusing all your funds on one investment would not be a wise move to make. It will not start your portfolio off positively, as you are making yourself more risk-averse. While not diversifying your portfolio at this point, it makes the most sense to start your portfolio off with a few investments at the onset to make your portfolio less risk-averse and lowering exposure to various market risks at the creation of your portfolio.

Let's say you have funded your account and purchased six different investments of various share amounts. The best course of action, in my opinion, would be to invest, with the $150 a month that was established in the earlier chapters of this book, half the investments you purchased for one month. Then the other half of investments for the next month. For example:

Portfolio:

Investment A, B, C, D, E, F.

Month 1:

Focus on buying shares in investment A, B, and C.

Month 2:

Focus on buying shares in investment D, E, and F.

Month 3:

Focus on buying shares in investment A, B, and C, and so on.

This would only need to last a few months into starting the portfolio. You would focus on doing things this way because you are trying to establish a solid base of investments. By building levels each month like this, you avoid building your investments one at a time, thereby making yourself less risk-averse and risk losing less wealth while your portfolio is in development.

Your introduction to diversification would have begun by the level-building strategy about investing in your portfolio for specific investments groupings in an alternating manner whenever you purchase your shares for the investments. To better understand it, we should take a deep dive into what diversification is and why it's essential to maintain your portfolio. *Diversification* is the practice of spreading your investments around so that your exposure to any one type of asset is limited. This practice is designed to help reduce the volatility of your portfolio over time. One of the keys to successful investing is learning how to balance your comfort level with risk against your time horizon for investing. Investing too conservatively at a young age can affect the growth of your portfolio. Conversely, investing too aggressively at an older age can expose you to market volatility at an age where you have less time and opportunity to recoup any losses. Having a diversified portfolio can help mitigate risk, but keep in mind diversification does not ensure a profit or guarantee your portfolio against losses.

Primary Components of a Diversified Portfolio

1. Domestic Stocks

Domestic stocks are the stocks of American companies traded on various stock exchanges. These represent the most aggressive investment of a portfolio and provide a high opportunity for long-term growth. A domestic stock's purpose is to split a company's ownership interest evenly across the number of shares outstanding for that company. Every shareholder owns a portion of the company, and their ownership interest is proportional to the number of shares they own compared to the total number of outstanding shares. This type of stock can be broken down into three subcategories of stocks:

Common Stock

- Common stock is the most readily available of the three and the only of the three types to grant voting rights to the shareholders in direct proportion to the number of shares owned.
- Common stock may or may not pay a dividend.

Preferred Stock

- Preferred stock almost always pays a dividend.
- When a company is profitable, preferred stockholders must get paid first.

Convertible Preferred Stock

- Convertible Preferred almost always pays a dividend.
- When a company is profitable, convertible preferred stockholders also get paid first.
- It can be converted to common stock if and when certain publicly disclosed conditions are met.

2. Bonds

A *bond* is a fixed-income instrument representing a loan made by an investor to a borrower (typically corporate or governmental). Interest rates and bond prices are inversely related: as rates rise, bond prices fall, and vice versa. Bonds have maturity dates which is when the principal must be paid in full or the borrower would risk default. They are generally considered less volatile than stocks. Bonds generally have lower growth potential than stocks but traditionally pay a fixed interest rate consistently.

3. Short-Term Investments

Short-term investments are financial investments that can be easily converted to cash, typically within five years. Many short-term investments can and may be converted or sold after three to twelve months and can include CDs (certificates of deposit), money market accounts, high yield savings accounts, government bonds, and treasury bills. These investments generally offer lower rates of return but are highly liquid and offer investors the flexibility to withdraw money quickly, if need be.

4. International Stocks

International stocks are stocks issued by non-US companies. They are instruments such as equities and bonds that provide US investors with access to a variety of global options that may have little link to US assets and each other. Mutual funds and ETFs are the most common ways for investors to participate in overseas markets. Generally, these stocks are very risky but potentially have excellent return rates for their higher risk. Investors can use these types of stocks to diversify the geographic and political risks associated with their portfolios.

Secondary Components of a Diversified Portfolio

1. Sector Funds

A *sector fund* is an investment fund that invests only in businesses that operate in a particular industry or sector of the economy. These types of funds are usually available as mutual funds or exchange-traded funds. These funds focus on a single sector in a market, making them less diverse and more volatile. Their performance is linked to the performance of the industry in which they invest. Sector funds allow investors to take targeted bets on the appreciation potential of a particular industry category.

2. Commodity-Focused Funds

Commodity-focused funds invest in raw materials or commodities, such as oil or wheat, mainly through futures contracts. A commodity ETF is usually focused on either a single commodity held in physical storage or investments in commodities futures contracts. While not in the scope of this book, here's a definition, so you at least know what the term means: a *futures contract* is a legal agreement to buy or sell a particular commodity asset or security at a predetermined price at a specified time in the future.

3. Real Estate Funds

A *real estate fund* is a mutual fund that invests in securities offered by public real estate companies, including REITs. This is also not in the scope of this book, but so you at least know what the term means, a *real estate investment trust (REIT)* is a corporation that invests in income-producing real estate and is bought and sold like a stock.

4. Asset Allocation Funds

Asset allocation funds are funds in balanced categories made up of a mix of stocks and bonds. These funds are set up to offer various financial goals depending on the account makeup and can include providing capital appreciation, income, and diversification. These funds are very popular retirement funds and are generally used in those funds as specific allocations for planned retirement date planning.

The primary goal of diversification isn't to maximize returns, but to limit volatility on the portfolio. There are two essential factors to consider for any financial goal someone chooses to undertake: first is the *time horizon*, or how long it will take until you need the money, second is the person's *risk tolerance.* The constant of the two, risk tolerance, factors more with risk-averse people whose comfort levels are based on the level of risk they feel they are facing. They can disregard time if they are in a situation they think will produce the best outcome. While the variable of the two, time horizon, factors more with people who feel they are a long way away from their financial goal and don't mind taking on more risk as they consider they have more time to recover from any losses they may occur. Regardless of your goal, time horizon, or risk tolerance, a diversified portfolio is the foundation of any smart investment strategy.

Robo-Advisors

Robo-Advisors are a newer technology being implemented by more brokers each day. What is a Robo-Advisor, also known as automated investing services? Well, to put it briefly, it's a relatively hands-off way to invest, using computer algorithms and advanced software to build and manage your investment portfolio. When you sign up for a Robo-Advisor account, the platform will ask you several questions about your investment objectives, time horizon, and risk tolerance.

The Robo-Advisor recommends one or more investment portfolios based on these characteristics, which commonly include low-cost ETFs. A Robo-Advisor could be an excellent alternative if you feel like you need some more investment advice. Annual Robo-Advisor fees can amount to 0.25 percent of your portfolio's worth, and you may also have to pay ETF cost ratios. Services can range from automatic portfolio rebalancing to tax optimization. *Rebalancing* is the process of realigning the weightings of a portfolio of assets.

Here are four ways to determine if a Robo-Advisor is right for you:

- **Type of Account** -- Most Robo-Advisors manage both individual retirement accounts and taxable accounts. Some also handle trusts, and some others can assist you with your 401(k).

- **Minimum Investment Requirements** - Some robo-advisors require $5,000 or more, but most have account minimums of $500 or less.
- **Portfolio Recommendations** - Robo-advisors generally offer five to ten portfolio choices based on your risk tolerance, goals, and investment preferences, usually determined from responses from a questionnaire. The service's algorithm will suggest a portfolio based on your responses to these questions, but you should be able to reject it if you prefer something else.
- **Investment Selection** - Robo-Advisors largely build their portfolios from low-cost ETFs, where you will still pay the funds' expense ratio fees plus the Robo-Advisor management fee.

(Benson, "11 Best Robo-Advisors of August," August 11, 2021)

Chapter Summary

- Diversification is the practice of spreading your investments around so that your exposure to any one type of asset is limited. This practice is designed to help reduce the volatility of your portfolio over time. A well-diversified portfolio is made up of both primary and secondary investments.
- The four primary components of a diversified portfolio are: domestic stock, bonds, short term investments, and international stock.
- The four secondary components of a diversified portfolio are: sector funds, commodity-focused funds, real estate funds, and asset allocation funds.
- There are two important factors you should consider for any financial goal you choose to undertake: the time horizon, or how long it will take until you need the money, and your risk tolerance.
- Robo-Advisors are a newer technology being implemented by more brokers each day. They use computer algorithms and advanced software to build and manage your investment portfolio.

Services can range from automatic portfolio rebalancing to tax optimization.

- Factors that determine if a Robo-Advisor is right for you are: the type of account you want, minimum investment requirements, portfolio recommendations, and the investment selection.

In this chapter, you learned much about starting your investment portfolio, types of stocks, diversification, and robo-advisors. In the next chapter, you will learn all about how many stocks you should own, the best ways to diversify your portfolio, and the importance of rebalancing.

6

HOW MANY ASSETS SHOULD YOU OWN

In "Risk Reduction and Portfolio Size," an article published in the *Journal of Business* back in 1977, researchers examined closely how the number of different shares in a portfolio could affect an investor's overall risk. For this survey, data was collated from a sample of 3,290 securities on the New York Stock exchange at the time, and portfolio sizes ranging from 1 to 200 different shares were compared to a portfolio, within which all the shares in its index were held equally. The researchers found that a portfolio of 10–20 stocks had significantly less risk than one with 4–6 stocks, with the risk score falling further as the number of stocks in the portfolio increased (Elton & Gruber).

While it may seem that many sources have diverse opinions on the "right" number of stocks to own in a portfolio, there is no one-size-fits-all answer to this question. Instead, the correct number of stocks to hold in your portfolio can depend on several factors, such as your country of residence and investment, investment time horizon, market conditions, and propensity to stay up-to-date with your portfolio. These factors, alongside diversification, can allow investors to reduce their exposure to unsystematic risk.

Unsystematic risk is defined as risk associated with or unique to a specific company or industry. It is the uncertainty that comes with investing in a company or sector. For example, a new rival in the market with the capacity to capture considerable market share from the company invested in, a legislative change (which could drive down company sales), a change in management, or a product recall are all examples of unsystematic risk. Conversely, *systematic risk* can be considered the probability of loss related to the entire stock market or index.

Unsystematic Risk

- This risk can be controlled and mitigated with diversification; key types are financial or business risk.
- Five types of this risk are financial, business, operational, strategic, and legal risk.
- Key examples of this risk include management inefficiency, flawed business model, liquidity issues, or worker strikes.

Systematic Risk

- While this risk is both unpredictable and impossible to avoid, it can be managed in a portfolio by including a variety of asset classes. Fixed income, cash, real estate, dividend, and so on, will each react differently to an event that affects the overall market.
- You can identify the systematic risk of a particular security or fund by looking at its beta. *Beta* measures how volatile an investment is compared to the overall market.

It can be tough to build a well-diversified portfolio of assets and stocks you are pleased with, especially for new investors. While there is no consensus on the answer, there is a reasonable range of stocks to hold in a portfolio. As a general rule, most investors hold between fifteen and twenty stocks, at the least. For quick and easy diversification in your portfolio without staying aware of so many stocks, appropriate investment vehicles might include *index funds*, *ETFs*, and *mutual funds*. These assets provide diversification across markets, sectors, and indexes that you can maintain and monitor more efficiently.

Index Funds

An ***index fund*** is a type of mutual fund or exchange traded fund (ETF) with a portfolio constructed to track the components of a financial market index, such as the Standard & Poor's 500 Index (S&P 500). These funds follow their benchmark index regardless of the state of the markets. Investing in an index fund is a form of passive investing.

Key Takeaways:

1. Index funds have lower expenses and fees than actively managed funds.
2. Index funds follow a passive investment strategy.
3. Index funds seek to match the risk and return of the market.
4. Portfolios of index funds only change when their benchmark indexes change.

Pros:

- Excel in diversification.
- Have a low expense ratio.
- Can have strong long-term returns.
- Ideal for buy and hold investors.

Cons:

- Vulnerable to market swings and crashes.
- Lack flexibility in the fund.
- Minimum human element.
- Limited gains.

In an *actively managed* fund, the portfolio manager actively picks stock and tries to time the market. *Timing the market* involves choosing securities to invest in and strategizing when to buy and sell them.

Key Takeaways:

1. Actively managed funds try to outperform their benchmark.
2. Actively managed funds generally have higher expense ratios than index funds. The *expense ratio* includes all the operating expenses of the fund.
3. Actively managed funds are not guaranteed to outperform their benchmark, with many failing to beat the market consistently.

Pros:

- Make it possible to beat the market index.
- Several funds have been known to post huge returns, though this performance changes over time.

Cons:

- Statistically, most actively managed funds underperform the market index.
- Fund management fees eat into any returns, therefore to be worthwhile investments, they have to outperform the market.
- Historical data is the only way to know how well a fund has done; there's no way to predict real-time performance.

Exchange-Traded Funds

An *ETF* is a class of fund that mimics an index, sector, commodity, or even another asset. It can be traded on the stock exchange. An ETF holds assets such as stocks, commodities, or bonds and trades close to its net asset value over the trading day. ETFs can be attractive as investments because of their low costs, tax efficiency, and stock-like features.

Key Takeaways:

1. ETF share prices fluctuate all day as the ETF is bought and sold.
2. ETFs can contain all types of investments, including stocks, bonds, or commodities; some offer only US holdings, while others are international.
3. ETFs offer low expense ratios and fewer broker commissions than buying stocks individually.
4. There are ETFs in just about every index or sector available to trade stocks.

Pros:

- Has access to many stocks across various industries.
- Generally have low expense ratios and fewer broker commissions.
- Diversification provides risk management for the fund.
- ETFs exist for targeted industries.

Cons:

- Single industry ETFs limit diversity.
- Lack of liquidity hinders transactions.
- ETFs are frequently promoted as low-cost vehicles for passive index investing, but not all ETFs have modest management fees or are managed passively.

An *actively managed ETF* will have a benchmark index, but managers may change sector allocations, market-time trades, or deviate from the index as they see fit. Although actively managed ETFs contain many characteristics of a traditional ETF, they still come at a premium. With higher expense ratios, there's pressure on fund managers to outperform the market.

Key Takeaways:

1. Does not adhere to passive investment strategy.
2. Actively managed ETFs have benchmark indexes, but managers may deviate from the index as they see fit.
3. Many actively managed ETFs have higher expense ratios which put pressure on fund managers to outperform the market.

Pros:

- An active manager can shift underperforming positions to more appropriate sectors.
- Funds have an opportunity for benchmark beating returns.

Cons:

- Higher expense ratios than traditional ETFs put pressure on fund managers to outperform the market.
- Funds may be less diversified than a traditional ETF.

Mutual Funds

A *mutual fund* is an investment that gathers money from investors to purchase stocks, bonds, and other assets. A mutual fund aims to create a more diversified portfolio than the average investor could do independently. A professional fund manager purchases a mutual fund's securities.

Key Takeaways:

1. Funds provide low-cost access to diverse, professionally managed portfolios for micro- and small-scale investors.
2. Mutual funds are classified according to the types of assets they invest in, their investing goals, and the sort of returns they target.

3. Mutual funds can have commissions and expense ratios that may affect the return.

4. Income is typically earned from a mutual fund in these areas. Dividends on stocks and interests on bonds are paid out as distributions. You sell securities that have increased in price as capital gains. Or, if the fund holdings increase in price but are not sold by the fund manager, the fund shares increase in price. You can then sell those shares for a profit.

Pros:

- Liquidity and diversification of the fund.
- Minimal investment requirements.
- Professional management of the fund.
- Variety of offerings by mutual funds.

Cons:

- High fees, commissions, and other expenses.
- Significant cash presence in portfolios.
- Funds have no Federal Deposit Insurance Corporation (FDIC) coverage.
- Difficulty in comparing funds.
- Lack of transparency in a fund's holding.

Mutual funds are divided into several categories, representing securities they have targeted for their portfolios and the type of returns they seek. These are the main types of mutual funds:

1. Stock (Equity) Funds

Stock funds typically carry the most significant risk as well as the greatest potential returns. Fluctuations in the stock market can drastically affect the returns on stock equity funds. There are various subcategories within this group, including growth funds, income funds, sector funds, aggressive growth funds, value funds, and so on. These funds often invest in equities issued by a diverse selection of companies from various US industries and economic sectors. Each type of fund tries to maintain a portfolio with specific characteristics.

2. Bond (Fixed-Income) Funds

Bond funds are typically less risky than stock funds. They focus on investments that pay a set rate of return, such as corporate bonds or government bonds. Bond funds are often actively managed and seek to buy relatively undervalued bonds to sell them at a profit. These mutual funds are likely to pay higher returns than certificates of deposit and money market investments, but bond funds aren't without risk. Because there are many different types of bonds, bond funds can vary dramatically depending on where they invest.

3. Balanced Funds

Stocks, bonds, money markets, and other investments are all part of the portfolio of a *balanced fund*. These funds are often a "fund of funds," investing in other mutual funds. Balanced funds are a one-stop destination for investors who want to invest in both equity and debt assets. The primary goal of these types of funds is to achieve a balanced risk-reward ratio and maximize profits on mutual fund investments. As a result, balanced or hybrid mutual funds are appropriate for investors seeking capital growth with little risk. An example would be a "target-date fund," which automatically chooses and reallocates assets based on a retirement target date.

4. Money Market Funds

These funds generally have the lowest returns because they carry the lowest risk. *Money market funds* typically consist of safe, short-term debt, treasury bills. Money market funds are managed with the purpose of maintaining a high level of asset stability through liquid investments while also providing dividends to investors. Usually, these are a safe place to put your money; you won't receive any substantial returns, but you also won't lose any principal.

5. Index Funds

Index funds are stock baskets that track a segment of the stock market, or the entire market in some situations. These funds are made up of assets that correspond with a major market index such as the Standard & Poor's (S&P 500) or the Dow Jones Industrial Average (DJIA), intending to mirror the risk and returns of that index.

6. Exchange-Traded Funds (ETFs)

An *exchange-traded fund* is a sort of investment fund that is also an exchange-traded product, meaning it can be bought and sold on stock markets. These funds can be traded like stocks but offer the diversification of mutual funds. ETFs can also be built to track certain investment strategies. Compared to mutual funds, ETFs tend to be more liquid and cost-effective.

7. Income Funds

Income funds attempt to provide steady income consistently. The funds invest primarily in government and high-quality corporate debt. The target audience for this type of fund is retirees or conservative investors. However, because they are income tax-conscious, investors may want to avoid these funds.

8. International/Global Funds

International funds invest only in assets located outside your home country. At the same time, global funds can invest in international funds and your home country. While not any riskier or safer than other domestic investments, these funds do tend to be more volatile based on the unique country and political risk.

9. Specialty Funds

These types of funds generally focus on targeted segments of the market or specific strategies. For example, there can be sector funds, which target particular sectors of the economy, such as financial, technology, real estate, and so on. In addition, there can be regional funds, which focus on specific geographic areas of the world. Finally, socially responsible funds invest in companies that meet specific guidelines, such as not investing in tobacco, weapons, and the like.

Modern Portfolio Theory

What is Modern Portfolio Theory? *Modern Portfolio Theory (MPT)* is a model that describes how risk-averse investors might build their holdings to optimize expected returns while considering a certain level of market risk. This style of investing can be helpful for investors trying to produce more efficient portfolios using ETFs. The portfolio's return is based on statistical measures, such as variance and correlation, making the individual investment less critical than affecting the entire portfolio. Today, MPT is a common strategy for constructing investment portfolios particularly as it is based on the concept of passive investing.

The MPT focuses on building investment portfolios with non-correlated assets, which means that if one item in a portfolio is severely impacted, other assets are not necessarily damaged as well. Diversification is based on this concept. For example, if an investor's portfolio includes both oil and technology stocks, and a new government rule on oil businesses reduces revenue, the oil stocks will lose value; however, the technology stocks will not be harmed. The gains in tech companies will more than make up for the losses in oil stocks.

The counter to this theory would be the *Post Modern Portfolio Theory (PMPT)*, an optimization theory that uses the downside risk of returns to determine the level of return. This comes into play because many long-term investors prefer to either boost their profits above and beyond what passive investing can provide, lower their risk in a more significant amount, or both. Both theories explain how hazardous assets should be priced and how diversity should be used by rational investors to achieve portfolio optimization. The difference between the two lies in each definition of risk and how that risk influences expected returns.

Rebalancing Your Portfolio

Your portfolio is balanced if it has been carefully built to meet your risk tolerance and investment goals. For instance, assuming you want to have 70 percent of your portfolio in stocks and 30 percent in bonds, if you fund your portfolio in this manner from the start, it would be a balanced portfolio. The issue is that these proportions in your portfolio do not remain constant over time. Going by this example, if the value of your stocks in your portfolio exceeds the value of your bonds, then your investment portfolio could be considered substantially out of balance.

Rebalancing is a trading strategy for bringing a portfolio back into line with its desired asset allocation once it has diverged. It entails buying and selling assets in a portfolio periodically to maintain your portfolio's original or targeted asset allocation or risk level. To rebalance your portfolio, you can either sell your high-performing investments, buy lower-performing ones, or strategically allocate new funds.

The most basic method of rebalancing is *calendar rebalancing*. This technique entails reviewing the portfolio's investment holdings at predefined time intervals and reverting to the prior allocation at a predetermined frequency. Weekly rebalancing would be too expensive, and a yearly strategy would allow for too much intermediate portfolio drift, thus monthly and quarterly assessments are often preferred. Time limits, transaction costs, and permitted drift must all be considered while determining the optimal rebalancing frequency.

Calendar rebalancing has a number of advantages to more responsive techniques, including the fact that it takes much less time and money for the investor because it includes fewer trades and occurs on predetermined dates. On the other hand, a notable disadvantage here is that calendar rebalancing does not allow for rebalancing at other times not specified, even if the market moves dramatically.

A *constant-mix strategy* with bands or corridors is a more responsive approach to rebalancing that focuses on the permissible percentage composition of an asset in a portfolio. A target weight and a tolerance range are assigned to each asset class or individual security.

For example, an allocation plan might mandate that 30 percent of assets be held in developing market equities, 30 percent in domestic blue chips, and 40 percent in government bonds, with a positive or negative 5 percent margin for each asset class. In general, emerging market and domestic blue chip holdings should be between 25 and 35 percent of the portfolio, while government bonds should be between 35 and 45 percent. The entire portfolio is rebalanced to match the initial target composition when the weight of any one holding moves outside of the permitted band.

Who Needs To Rebalance?

Most investors who own stocks, bonds, mutual funds, or other assets in any combination of retirement or brokerage accounts will need to rebalance at some point or another. That being said, you should aim to rebalance your portfolio at least once a year, even if you're a passive buy and hold investor.

Why Do You Need To Rebalance?

Well-formed portfolios maintain a mix of diverse asset classes. These can include stocks, bonds, real estate, and so on. Assets with rising prices account for a larger share of a portfolio's overall worth over time, whereas assets with falling values account for a smaller share. Rebalancing restores the investor's desired weighting of various assets within the portfolio by selling assets that have increased in value and buying assets that have decreased in value.

In addition, within the various asset classes of your investments, there should be diversification. These safeguards help protect your portfolio from risk while keeping you on track to meeting your target financial goals.

Continuing with the example above, you can either sell some of your stock investments and put the money into bonds or buy more bonds to realign your asset allocation with your risk tolerance. In addition, you can rebalance your portfolio at a specific time interval (say, yearly), or you can rebalance only when your portfolio becomes manifestly unbalanced. For example, if your original risk tolerance led you to put 60 percent of your money in bonds, your rebalanced portfolio should contain 60 percent bonds as well.

Chapter Summary

- While financial experts believe that a well-diversified portfolio should hold at least twenty stocks, the appropriate number of stocks for your portfolio depends on a number of factors. These include: your country of residence and investment, your investment time horizon, prevailing market conditions, your financial goals, and your ability to stay up-to-date on your holdings.
- You can achieve a well-diversified investment portfolio by investing in index funds, ETFs and mutual funds.
- Modern Portfolio Theory (MPT) is a theory on how risk-averse

investors can construct portfolios to maximize expected returns based on a given level of market risk. This style of investing can be helpful for investors trying to produce more efficient portfolios using ETFs. The counter to this theory would be the Post Modern Portfolio Theory (PMPT), an optimization theory that uses the downside risk of returns to determine the level of return.

- Rebalancing is a trading strategy for bringing a portfolio back into line with its desired asset allocation once it has diverged. It entails buying and selling assets in a portfolio periodically to maintain your portfolio's original or targeted asset allocation or risk level.

In this chapter, you learned about how many stocks you should own, the importance of diversification for your portfolio, the Modern and Post Modern Portfolio theories, and portfolio rebalancing. In the next chapter you will learn how to know when to sell your stocks and how to know when to hold.

7

HOW TO KNOW WHEN TO SELL YOUR STOCKS

There is a story of a lazy man who was a good friend to a king. As they strolled through the king's garden one afternoon, the lazy man began to lament about his woes to the king: "All my relatives avoid me and label me lazy. I have tried several times to get a proper job, but nobody wants my services. My enemies seem to have told everyone that I have no value for time, and I never do anything worthwhile at the right time." He cried.

"So let's make a deal," said the king. "If you can present yourself today at my treasury, right before sunset, whatever gold, pearls, or precious stones you touch will all be yours." The man was blown away by his friend's generosity and rushed home to share the news with his wife. At the end of his narration, the woman listened and told him, "Go and get the gold and gems now. If you leave right away, you will get to the royal treasury at the right time."

As the story goes, the lazy man sat down, already too tired to make the journey back, and said, "I can't go now, give me lunch first." He had his lunch and, afterward, decided to take a nap and so overslept. When he woke up, he hurriedly picked a few bags and set off for the king's treasury. He finally reached the palace around nighttime and was met with the palace gates, tightly shut. Aside from his laziness, he lost the chance of a lifetime because he didn't know the value of doing things at the right time.

In theory, the ability to make money in the stock market depends on two important decisions: buying assets at the right time, and then selling those assets at the right time. To make a profit these decisions should be made with a level of synergy that will be profitable. If you don't sell at the right time, the benefits of having bought at the right time very quickly disappear. Buying stocks and researching which ones to buy can be exciting for many individuals. On the other hand, human nature might make it difficult for us to sell shares, regardless of whether they have created profits or losses. As a result, it can be a difficult decision to make. If you're unsure whether to sell a stock for profit or at a loss, consider the following guidelines.

Reasons To Sell Stock

We put a lot of emphasis on investment decisions, with importance on buying. However, the selling aspect of investing is just as important as buying and can make the difference between success and failure. So let's consider some reasons for selling a stock or asset.

Lack of Margin of Safety

The *margin of safety* is an investment concept that asserts that investors should only buy securities if their market price is much lower than their true worth. The margin of safety of an investment is the difference between the market price of a security and your estimate of its intrinsic value. Your goal as the investor is to pay less than the actual value. Owning stocks that heavily favor you winning over the market overwhelmingly works in your favor. If the stock price rises to the point where it can't be held with a margin of safety, then the stock should be sold.

Five Percent Rule

The *five percent rule* is an investment concept that states that an investor should not invest more than 5 percent of their portfolio funds into a single security or investment. The five percent rule serves as a guideline rather than a requirement. The rationale for this rule is simple: diversification can almost completely remove company-specific risk. Allowing single stock positions to grow too large exposes you to risk for which you will not be reimbursed. It doesn't specify how much you should put in, though, because it depends on your stock research and knowledge.

Fundamentals Change/Loss of Faith in the Company

The fundamentals of a company can change after you purchase some stock of that company. The company may have had a change in leadership. There may be declining profit margins or decreased revenue, legal issues, an increase in competition, or more issues. If these changes affect your margin of safety at the stock's current price, you may need to consider selling off your positions. Depending on the issue, you should determine whether the changes at hand are short-term and will work themselves out shortly, or appear to be more long-term sustained business changes.

Opportunity Cost

Opportunity cost is when the cost of one decision comes at the expense of making another. Opportunity cost refers to the amount of money you can lose if you buy one asset instead of another when it comes to investing. Regardless of performance, it's wise and possibly more profitable to explore other investments for your money. Being objective with your portfolio and its performance should override any emotional attachment with a stock position.

Stock Is Overpriced

The price-earning ratio helps investors determine if a stock is valued appropriately based on its current price and earnings per share. It is based on the company's past and future earnings, and a higher price-to-earnings ratio means that the stock price is high compared to company earnings and, as such, may be overvalued. Checking historical ratios can be helpful in checking a stock's valuation as well.

Need for Liquidity

An unforeseen but necessary need for liquidity also counts as a good reason to sell a stock. Stocks are assets, and there are times when people need to cash in on their assets. Whatever the reason, it would be wise to evaluate your portfolio to determine which assets to hold and sell in this situation.

Avoidance of Capital Gains Tax

When investors purchase stocks, not in a retirement account, any gains are subject to a capital gains tax. *Capital gains taxes* are taxes paid on profits from selling investments. These taxes don't apply to "tax-advantaged accounts" such as 401(k) plans, IRA plans, and 529 college education accounts.

Portfolio Adjustments

You may need to sell some stocks in your portfolio to rebalance them from time to time. As discussed previously, rebalancing your portfolio is an essential practice for various good reasons. For one, it allows you to review assets you've invested in and to confirm your positions are still meeting the goals you have for the portfolio.

Reasons Not To Sell a Stock

Knee-jerk reactions to the price movement of stocks you own are not good reasons to sell a stock. Whether the change is a dip or spike in the stock price, the price movement alone may give a complete picture of the value of the stock. While these situations can sometimes be determined as panic moves, more often, it is a case of trying to time the market. *Timing the market* involves predicting when the market will go up or down and buying or selling in investments to try and turn a profit. Market timing is viewed as a strategy that doesn't work and won't produce consistent positive returns. For the average investor, you should avoid market timing and instead focus on investing with a long-term strategy.

Common Mistakes Selling Stocks

In the stock market, as in life, nothing is a sure thing. Mistakes can be made when selling assets that can be avoidable when we know what to look for and how to address things when we see them happening. Let's address some of the mistakes that can be made and how to avoid making them.

Panic Behavior

Everyone knows decisions made because of fear or scarcity are some of the worst ways to make a decision, and if you don't, you should, as it is not a wise way to live. The stock market can be highly uncertain during bear markets or market corrections. A *bear market* is a period of falling stock prices, typically by 20 percent or more. Investor confidence is low, and investing can be viewed as riskier during this period. If you are a long-term investor and nothing with the company has changed during this time, this would be one of the worst times to sell—the bottom. During the 2008–09 recession, the Dow Jones lost half of its value in less than a year. Millions of investors saw billions of dollars in assets disappear, with many pulling out with their investments in losing positions.

What to do instead:

Five years later, from the 2009 market bottom, the Dow Jones rose roughly 10,000 points to a new record. Of course, the stock market doesn't always bounce back so drastically, but it does bounce back. The winners here were the investors who were patient with their investments, utilizing a buy and hold strategy. While mentioned in earlier chapters, we can define it here as a passive investment strategy in which an investor buys stocks (or other types of securities such as ETFs) and holds them for an extended period regardless of fluctuations in the market. An investor who uses a buy and hold strategy selects investments, but has no concern for short-term price movements.

Loss Aversion Bias

Loss aversion is a characteristic of investor behavior in which investors would rather avoid a loss than possibly earn good returns. It is common to want to breakeven on an investment. Loss aversion may cause an investor to hold stock even when they believe that they should sell it. Rather than being actual behavior, this relates to the mindset that can create behavior.

For instance, let's assume Sarah purchased a stock for $100 and three months later decided to sell

the stock due to a fundamental change in the company's outlook. The price of the stock is now $97. As you might imagine, Sarah doesn't want to take any loss, so she decides to wait until the stock

reaches $100 in hopes that she can then breakeven and avoid a loss. Therefore, her potential reward for holding the stock is only $3 because she has decided to sell at $100. She has decided to risk $97 for the potential of making $3 more than she can receive today. Her mindset on losing $3 has caused her to make a poor risk/reward decision.

<u>What to do instead:</u>

The best course of action is to train your thinking to make the most rational decision possible. Whatever decision you make needs to be made with reason from research, and conviction that the decision is the best one going forward. Then, once a decision is made, stick with that decision and move forward, letting the consequences be what they may be, whether positive or negative.

Short-Term Thinking

Should investors sell stock after it drops a certain amount below the price paid? Some people can't stand the pain of a falling stock price. To stop the bleeding, investors try to use strategies such as stop/loss orders. *Stop/loss orders* are buying/selling rules set up in your portfolio to buy or sell a stock once the price reaches a specified price, known as the *stop price*. Investors use these orders to limit losses when the price of investment decreases (if the investor is long) or when the price of an investment increases (if the investor is short). *Value investors*, or investors that buy and hold investments, should never sell a stock because the price falls. This is because these price dips are usually short-term in nature. However, the nature of investing indicates it should be for the long term, or else you would be a day trader.

<u>What to do instead:</u>

In the short term, the stock market is risky. Thinking as a value investor will produce the best results long term. Being patient will be a common theme among things to do to avoid selling mistakes. Taking a long-term mindset no matter how the market is acting will make the market much less risky. This would be the best time to buy into a stock when the price dips.

When To Hold Your Stocks

Your investment strategy plays a significant role in how you hold your stocks. The tax rate on long-term capital gains (stocks owned for longer than one year) is much lower than short-term capital gains. Knowing when to hold stocks can be less confusing when an investor researches company health, overall market conditions, and their own financial needs as they relate to personal short-term and long-term goals. Zeroing in on the critical information helps them avoid making a rash decision.

Chapter Summary

- In the stock market, buying at the right price may determine the profit gained, but selling at the right price guarantees the profit (if any). You sell stock through the execution of a stock sale order and these include: market sell order, limit sell order, stop limit sell order, sell stop-loss order.
- Good reasons to sell your stock include the following: loss of faith in the company, overpriced stock, adherence to the 5% rule, a need for liquidity, avoidance of capital gains tax, and portfolio readjustment.
- Common mistakes to avoid when selling stock include: loss aversion bias, selling solely because the stock price has fallen, and failure to exit a losing investment.
- When your stock value plunges, the key is to research extensively and then ask yourself if any experienced investor would consider your asset worth buying at its current price. If it is, it would be wise to hold your stock longer. If your answer is no, then you would be selling at the right time.

In this chapter, you learned about stock investments, portfolio diversification, and how to know when to sell your stock. In the last chapter of this book, you will learn how to generate earnings on your investment returns through the process of compounding.

8

COMPOUNDING

*"Compound interest is the eighth wonder of the world.
He who understands it, earns it; he who doesn't, pays it."*

— ALBERT EINSTEIN

If I gave you a penny every day in January, at the end of the month, you'd have thirty-one cents. Now, what if I gave you one penny the first day and two pennies the next? Then on the third day, I doubled it to four pennies, and on the fourth day, I doubled it again to eight pennies, and so on until the end of the month. How much money do you think you'd have? You'd end up with 2.1 billion cents. That's a billion with a *b*. The basic idea here is that when you invest money, it earns interest or rises in value. In your second year of investing, you earn interest on both your original money and the interest from the previous year. Then, you earn interest on your original money and the interest from the previous two years in the third year. And so forth. It's like rolling a snowball down a snowy hill: it will build on itself and get larger and larger until it sets off an avalanche.

Factors That Affect Your Gains When Compounding

Compounding is the process of generating earnings from prior earnings. It is the system through which an asset generates returns that are then reinvested or invested in, creating their profits to multiply overall investment gains. It acts on both assets and liabilities and is known as "interest on interest." To function optimally, compounding requires four major factors:

1. The principal sum remaining invested.
2. Earnings or dividend reinvestment.
3. Regularly paid interests.
4. Time sufficiency.

The Principal Sum Remaining Invested

Your principal is your initial investment sum paid for an asset, security, or bond, and this does not include any interests derived. It is the starting point for calculating the first interest payment and should remain invested because compounding works by increasing your principal along with all earnings on it. For example, assume you invest $100 (the principal) at a 5 percent annual interest rate. When you multiply the principal by the interest rate, you get a $5 interest payment. After the first year, you will have $105 if you earn 5 percent interest compounded annually. If you keep this investment for another year, you will be paid interest on both the original $100 and the $5 in interest you earned the first year. It makes no difference whether you are an experienced investor; investing regularly and staying invested for an extended period will help you reap the most benefits of compounding.

Earnings or Dividend Reinvestment

Investors can significantly increase their annual returns and total assets by methodically reinvesting dividend income in these high-quality stocks. Reinvesting your earnings or dividends compounds them more effectively and boosts your long-term returns. This is because your dividends will buy you more shares, which will subsequently raise your dividend value, allowing you to buy even more shares, and so on. You can accelerate the power of long-term compounding in your investment and retirement accounts by reinvesting your dividends. Also, if you own stock or mutual fund shares, you may be able to reinvest your dividends in additional shares. This keeps your investment base growing, allowing you to compound your return. It's putting your newfound money to work for you.

Regular Interest Payments

When the interest on your principal compounds, your balance increases. Interest is a payment made on the sum of your original investment. It can be compounded at any time, from continuously to daily to annually. There are two types of interest: simple interest and compound interest.

Simple interest is a sum of money payable on the principal or the initial deposit alone. It does not compound, and so the investor will only earn interest on the principal. Simple interest is paid out as earned and does not become part of an account's interest-bearing balance.

Compound interest, for its part, is the payment made or calculated by both the starting sum and the accumulated interests on it. Thus, it is the interest paid on the interest as well as the principal. This means that even if you never add another dollar to that original deposit, the money in the account will still grow exponentially over time. This means your total profit from capital gains, dividends, and interest payments for stock and bond investments. Compounding interests should be made regularly. This could be annually, semiannually, quarterly, monthly, or daily, depending on the nature of your investment account. A higher and regularly paid interest rate will contribute to a more substantial compounding rate on your investments.

Sufficiency of Time

Warren Buffett is one of the world's wealthiest men, but the vast majority of his net worth has accrued in his final years of life. He amassed a net worth of $1 billion over 56 years. After that, it took him only 27 years to turn that $1 billion into over $60 billion, thanks mainly to compound interest. Since 1988, Jim Simons, the hedge fund Renaissance Technologies founder, has compounded money at 66 percent each year. No one comes close to matching this achievement. Buffett's returns compounded at a rate of around 22 percent per year, or about a third of the rate. Still, Simons's net worth is estimated to be over $23 billion, meaning he is just 72 percent as wealthy as Buffett. Why is there such a disparity if Simons is such a superior investor? Because it took Simons until he was 50 years old to find his investment stride. He hasn't had nearly as much time to compound as Buffett. Simons would be worth $63,900,781,780,748,160,000 if he achieved his 66 percent annual returns during the 70 years Buffett has grown his fortune.

The more time you give your money to compound, the more it grows. Understanding the time value of money is critical for calculating the future value of money. In other words, a specific dollar amount today is worth more than the same dollar amount in the future. This is due to the impact of inflation. The longer an investment is allowed to compound, the higher the potential return. This explains why compound interest is essential for new investors. The sooner an investor starts saving, the greater their returns will be in the future.

Compounding is a great way to grow your finances, but it isn't without its unique risks. Below are the benefits as well as disadvantages of compounding:

Pros:

- With patience and investments that earn a regular interest rate, your capital will grow pretty quickly.
- If done correctly, dividend investing can triple your compounding benefits. When you reinvest dividends back into the market, buying more shares with the money you've made, you will earn more in the long run than if you simply collect dividend money and put it in your pockets.
- You can make better investment comparisons and financial decisions if you understand how compounding works.

Cons:

- When it comes to loans, the interest that accrues on the initial principal can be challenging to bear. Compounding can help you grow your earnings, but it can also balloon your debt if left unchecked.
- Compound interest is taxable, so any accrued interest will be taxed at your regular income tax rate unless you invest in a tax-deferred account.
- Compound interest can be challenging to calculate because it is calculated differently depending on the type of financial instrument, the rate used (APR or APY), and the number of compounding years.

Knowing how compounding works can dictate how you can best approach any investment opportunity to achieve the best return possible. Following some easy-to-follow guidelines can go a long way to building upon the growth of the account.

Invest Early

Early investing will aid in the accumulation of wealth to achieve long-term objectives. The earlier you start investing or saving, the less risk you will need to tolerate, and the more money you will stand to make over time.

Regular Deposits

While periodic or systematic investing does not guarantee a profit or protect against loss, adding to your investments regularly, such as monthly or weekly, can help you build wealth quickly. The accumulation serves as the foundation for calculating your interest.

Know Your Rate

Make sure you have reasonable interest rates, because a higher annual compound interest rate implies higher returns. Also, follow up with your broker to ensure that all interests are paid when due.

Be Patient

The power of compounding lies in the fact that it increases your gains, but this is majorly determined by time.

Common Compounding Mistakes To Avoid

We fail to grasp that even small amounts invested early in life can grow into large amounts later. Developing positive habits and avoiding these negative behaviors allows us to avoid pitfalls that can cost thousands of dollars.

Having no plan: Not having a plan will delay your progress in reaching your compounding objectives. If you don't set aside a regular time to review your portfolio and make sure that the value of the compounding assets has not changed, you might be in for a shock in the long run. A plan will assist you in determining your asset allocation for short- and long-term goals. This should be as specific and realistic as possible. It should also be reviewed periodically.

Failure to pay attention to hidden fees: When compounding, a seemingly insignificant fee or charge can add up to a lot of money over a few years. For example, two investments may carry similar risk and expected return, but one may have higher fees—all else equal, the fees would affect your returns. Therefore, it is critical to understand the fees you pay when investing because they reduce your return. Consult your broker or your financial advisor. Ask questions and weigh your options carefully.

Ignoring the tax rate: When you ignore the taxation policy on your interest while compounding, you might end up growing your earnings over a long time frame only to have a good portion of it taken away by the IRS. Fortunately, you can compound your interest and avoid paying more tax than necessary by using a tax-deferred account.

A *tax-deferred account* is an account that safeguards your earnings by allowing them to grow in your account tax-free until withdrawn. This restores the power of compounding to you, as your investment has the potential to grow faster without being hampered by taxes. In addition, if you don't have to pay taxes at all, or only until the end of the compounding period, rather than at the end of each year, you'll end up with far more money.

This is why tax-deferred accounts like the traditional IRA, Roth IRA, 401(k), SEP-IRA, and other tax-deferred IRAs are so important. For instance, if your investment account is an Individual Retirement Account, you would not have to pay taxes on the interest you earn until a later date, usually at or after the age of 59 years. Your income tax is also generally lower when you retire, so even then, you would end up paying less.

Whatever amount of money you can afford to invest for the long term, fund your investment account with it today. Time is your friend here. The longer you give interest to compound, the more substantial your gains will be.

Chapter Summary

- Compounding is the process of generating earnings from prior earnings. It is the system through which an asset generates returns, which are then reinvested or remain invested with the purpose of creating their own earnings to multiply the overall investment gains.
- To function optimally, compounding requires four major factors: the principal sum remaining invested, earnings or dividend reinvestment, regularly paid interests and the sufficiency of time.
- To compound effectively, you can apply the following tips: invest early, make regular deposits, ensure you have good interest rates, and finally, be patient.
- There are three common mistakes you should avoid when compounding. These include: having no plan, being inattentive to hidden fees, and ignoring the tax rates on your interest.
- You can compound your interest and avoid paying more tax than necessary by using a tax-deferred account. A tax-deferred account is an account that safeguards your earnings by allowing them to grow in your account tax-free until withdrawn.

FINAL WORDS

Our financial goals are different, but for the most part, one thing they share in common is that we are all constantly striving to increase our wealth and have more financial freedom. When we specify what we want for our finances, we can direct our investments in the best direction to get to our goals quicker. Whether or not you were born into wealth, you can achieve your financial breakthrough, but this will only be possible when we take responsibility for our financial habits, save as much as possible, and invest intelligently.

We learn best through practice and experience. There is no one perfect strategy to achieve a financial breakthrough. But what we can learn from this book is that our goals are valid and can be achieved once we commit fully to seeing them through and integrating the lessons from this book into the financial aspect of our life. Success means accomplishments as the result of our efforts and abilities. Proper preparation is the key to our success in life. How we think is how we act.

Regardless of your income today, you can always change your financial situation. The more you practice these financial principles in saving and investing money, the more you can provide for what we all desire—better living experiences for the future.

Summary of Principles to Achieving Your Financial Breakthrough

1. How Much You Should Invest

No matter how much you earn, the amount you invest yearly should be based on goals you want to achieve. Your investment goals give you not just a target to shoot towards, but also the drive to stick to your investment strategy. Your investment goal should also be practical and is best determined by the amount of money you have available to invest. What you should invest in and how much you should invest depends on your income, age, risk tolerance, and investing objectives.

2. Get Ready To Begin Investing

Get your finances in order so you can better determine how to start investing. Being ready isn't about racing against time to see how fast you can get it all done. It's far more essential to focus on doing things right by learning how to pace yourself. The best thing you can do before investing your money in any venture is to ensure that your finances are in order. Having your finances in order before you start investing will motivate you to not stop, and persevere if issues arise. You can get ready to begin investing by integrating certain practices into your life today. You could start an emergency fund, work towards investing an initial sum of $150 dollars each month or pay yourself first from your salary before fulfilling any other financial obligations.

3. How To Know Which Stock To Buy

There are so many stock options available for you to choose from on your investment journey, all with their different benefits and associated risks. Doing your homework on stocks you want to invest in and staying up to date with current news and information sets the basis for you to make informed decisions on what to buy. Research should be your ally here and before buying a stock, research extensively on the company, focusing on the following seven criteria: trends in the earnings and growth of the company, the company's strengths in relation to its peers, the company's debt to equity ratio, its price to earnings ratio, its dividend policy, the effectiveness of the leadership team, and long-term strength and stability of the company.

4. Where To Buy Stock

The type of investor you discover you are and the type of investing features you find most important will lead you to where to best buy your stocks. When you want to buy stock in a company, you'll need the services of a broker as well as your own brokerage account. Today, almost all forms of investing are done online. Finding the best online broker for you as a beginner can vary depending on your specific needs and preferences. For example, do you prefer a complex and full-featured stock trading platform, or would a simple, user-friendly app be enough? To help facilitate your decision on which broker may work best for you, the six current discount broker choices that I would encourage you to consider are: TD Ameritrade, Fidelity, E*Trade, Vanguard, Webull, and Ally Invest. These brokers offer full suites of services, account types, and investments allowing you to do just about anything on their platform and all for little or no commission on most of their major products.

5. Starting a Portfolio

When it's time to put all the savings you've made and research you've done into action, don't forget to diversify your portfolio. With the initial funding of your portfolio, a good plan of action would be to spread that funding over all the investments you plan on funding, initially at least. When starting your portfolio, focusing all your funds on one investment would not be a wise move to make. A better step would be to fund half of the assets you acquired for one month with the $150 per month set aside in the earlier chapters of this book. Then the second half of that for the following month's investments. Diversification matters a great deal for your portfolio because it helps you spread your investments across different asset classes to minimise your exposure to any one type of asset. Primary and secondary assets are the hallmarks of a well-diversified portfolio and the sooner you diversify, the quicker you can lower your portfolio's volatility over time.

6. How Many Stocks Should You Own

It can be tough to build a well-diversified portfolio of assets and stocks you are pleased with, especially for new investors. While there is no "correct" number of stocks and assets to own at any given time, there is a reasonable range of stocks to hold in a portfolio. As a general rule, most investors hold between fifteen and twenty stocks, at the least. For quick and easy diversification in your portfolio without staying aware of so many stocks, index funds, ETFs, and mutual funds may be appropriate investment vehicles. These assets provide diversification across markets, sectors, and indexes that you can maintain and monitor more efficiently. Also, you want to make sure you never allocate more than 5 percent of your portfolio to any one stock. Rebalancing or readjusting your portfolio is a great strategy here because it helps you bring your portfolio back into line with its desired asset allocation once it has diverged. It entails buying and selling assets in a portfolio periodically to maintain your portfolio's original or targeted asset allocation or risk level. To rebalance your portfolio, you can either sell your high-performing investments, buy lower-performing ones, or strategically allocate new funds.

7. How To Know When To Sell your Stock

The idea is to buy low and sell high, so it pays to stay on top of your stocks' value to determine whether the valuation justifies the price. Your ability to make money in the stock market depends on both buying and selling assets at the right time. If you don't sell at the right time, the benefits of having bought at the right time very quickly disappear. There are several good reasons to sell your stocks or assets and they include the following: loss of faith in the company, overpriced stock, adherence to the 5 percent portfolio rule, a need for liquidity, avoidance of capital gains tax, and a need to readjust your investment portfolio. To know when to hold, research the company health and the overall market conditions. Also, make time to review your own financial needs as relates to personal short-term and long-term goals. Zeroing in on this critical information is the best way to avoid a rash decision to sell off stock when it would serve you better to hold.

8. Compounding

Compounding is the process of generating earnings from prior earnings. Interest is often accumulated on a monthly, quarterly, semiannual, or annual basis. Compounding is the process of making money from an asset's earnings that have been reinvested. With continual compounding, any income you earn starts earning interest on itself right away. The power of compounding (sometimes known as compound interest) has the ability to turn your spare cash into an income generator. To compound effectively, invest early, make regular deposits, ensure you have good interest rates, and finally, be patient.

THANK YOU

Thank you for taking the time to read *Achieving Your Financial Breakthrough*. I hope this book has inspired you to take control of your financial situation for yourself and future generations.

If you have enjoyed reading this book or it has helped you in any way, please leave a comment where you bought this book so that it may help someone else. Please be honest with your review on how this book has or has not helped you on your journey.

REFERENCES

Ally Invest. "Investing With Us." [Web Page]. n.d. https://www. ally.com/invest.

AMG Funds. "The Effect of Compounding." Accessed June 18, 2021. https:// www.amgfunds.com/research_and_insights/investment_essentials/ practical/the-effect-of-compounding.html.

Becker, Matt. "Don't Let These Fears Stop You From Investing." *The Simple Dollar*. Last Modified April 3, 2020. https://www.thesimpledollar.com/ investing/too-many-millennials-are-afraid-of-investing/.

Beers, Brian. "11 ETF Flaws Investors Should Not Overlook." *Investopedia*. Last Modified January 6, 2021. https://www.investopedia.com/articles/ mutualfund/07/etf_downside.asp.

Benson, Alana. "11 Best Robo-Advisors of August 2021." *NerdWallet*. August 11, 2021. https://www.nerdwallet.com/best/investing/robo-advisors.

Best, Richard. "I Make $50k a Year; How Much Should I Invest?" *Investopedia*. Last Modified June 29, 2021. https://www.investopedia.com/articles/ personal-finance/022216/i-make-50k-year-how-much-should-i-invest.asp.

Better Life Coaching Blog. "The Kid In A Candy Store—A Story About Making Decisions." April 11, 2016, accessed June 10, 2021. https://www. google.com/amp/s/betterlifecoachingblog.com/2016/04/11/the-kid-in-a-candy-store-a-story-about-making-decisions/amp/.

Boyte-White, Claire. "The Complete Guide To Choosing An Online Stock Broker." *Investopedia*. Last Modified June 29, 2021. https://www.investopedia. com/investing/complete-guide-choosing-online-stock-broker/.

Carlson, Debbie. "8 Reasons To Sell a Stock or Fund." *US News: Money*. April 25, 2019. https://money.usnews.com/investing/stock-market-news/ slideshows/8-reasons-to-sell-a-stock-or-fund?slide=4.

Chen, James. "Compounding." *Investopedia*. Last Modified February 23, 2021. https://www.investopedia.com/terms/c/compounding.asp.

Chen, James. "Exchange Traded Funds (ETFs)." *Investopedia*. Last Modified March 3, 2021. https://www.investopedia.com/terms/e/etf.asp.

Coombes, Andrea, and Voigt, Kevin. "Vanguard Review 2021: Pros, Cons and How It Compares." *NerdWallet*. June 24, 2021. https://www.nerdwallet. com/reviews/investing/brokers/vanguard.

Corporate Finance Institute. "What Is An Investment Portfolio?" n.d., accessed June 17, 2021. https://corporatefinanceinstitute.com/resources/ knowledge/trading-investing/investment-portfolio/.

Davis, Chris. "Webull Review 2021: Pros, Cons and How It Compares." *Nerd-Wallet*. June 24, 2021. https://www.nerdwallet.com/reviews/investing/ brokers/webull.

Ellen, Rachel. "9 Inspiring Financial Stories." You Need a Budget [Blog]. January 14, 2021. https://www.youneedabudget.com/9-inspiring-financial-stories/.

Elton, Edwin, and Gruber, Martin. "Risk Reduction and Portfolio Size: An Analytical Solution." *The Journal of Business* 50, no. 4 (February 1977): 415–437.

https://www.researchgate.net/
publication/24102674_Risk_Reduction_and_Portfolio_Size_An_Analytical_S
olution.

E*Trade. "New To Online Investing." [Web Page]. n.d. https://us.
etrade.com/planning.

Farley, Alan. "Figure out Your Investment Goals." *Investopedia*. Last Modified October 29, 2020. https://www.investopedia.com/investing/figure-out-
your-investment-goals/.

Farrington, Robert. "15 Ways To Save An Extra $500 Per Month." *The College
Investor*. Last Modified May 2, 2021. https://thecollegeinvestor.com/16433/
save-more-money-each-month/.

Faulkenbery, Ken. "Selling A Stock: Good Reasons and Common Mistakes."
Arbor Investment Planner. Accessed June 18, 2021. https://www.
arborinvestmentplanner.com/selling-a-stock-good-reasons-common-
mistakes/.

Fernando, Jason. "Guide To Index Fund Investing." *Investopedia*. Last Modified February 4, 2021. https://www.investopedia.com/terms/i/indexfund.asp.

Fernando, Jason. "Opportunity Cost." *Investopedia*. Last Modified December
27, 2020. https://www.investopedia.com/terms/o/opportunitycost.asp.

Fidelity. "The Fidelity Advantage." [Web Page]. n.d. https://www.fidelity.
com/why-fidelity/overview.

Fidelity. "Why Diversification Matters." [Web Page]. n.d., accessed June 15,
2021. https://www.fidelity.com/learning-center/investment-products/
mutual-funds/diversification.

Fierbert, Andrew. "Investment Beginners 101: What Is Investing and Why
Does it Matter?" Listen Money Matters. January 2, 2021. https://www.
listenmoneymatters.com/investing-for-beginners/.

Finance Buzz. "23 Legit Ways To Make Extra Cash." Last Modified August 17,
2021. https://financebuzz.com/ways-to-make-extra-money?utm_source=
GoogleAdWords&utm_medium=paid-search-g&utm_campaign=

US_SideHustle_ROAS_6523447166_117262098687&utm_content=
481532220393&utm_term=make%20money%20online&mt=b&device=c&
devicemodel=&targetid=kwd-301080519511&target=&keyword=make%
20money%20online&campaignid=6523447166&adgroupid=117262098687&
gclid=CjwKCAjw1uiEBhBzEiwAO9B_Hfp1Ch6Jn8eyLZnebVKwSwVX-
OFqErKtuF6lFWZzWZAPUWnTdMFUHxoCezQQAvD_BwE.

Fontinelle, Amy. "How To Adjust and Renew Your Portfolio." *Investopedia.*
Last Modified January 24, 2020. https://www.investopedia.com/investing/
how-renew-and-adjust-your-portfolio/.

Fontinelle, Amy. "How To Set Financial Goals For Your Future." *Investopedia.* Last Modified March 29, 2021. https://www.investopedia.com/articles/
personal-finance/100516/setting-financial-goals/.

Frankel, Matt. "Ally Invest Review: Great For Diverse Investing Needs and
Much More." *The Ascent.* May 3, 2021. https://www.fool.com/the-ascent/
buying-stocks/ally-invest-review/.

Frankel, Matt. "Best Online Stock Brokers For Beginners For August 2021."
The Ascent. Last Modified August 2, 2021. https://www.fool.com/the-ascent/
buying-stocks/best-online-stock-brokers-beginners/.

Frankel, Matt. "Fidelity Review: Top Broker With Extensive Research
Tools." *The Ascent.* Last Modified April 16, 2021. https://www.fool.com/the-
ascent/buying-stocks/fidelity-review/.

Furhmann, Ryan. "When To Buy and When To Sell A Stock: 5 Tips."
Investopedia. Last Modified April 22, 2021. https://www.investopedia.com/
financial-edge/0412/5-tips-on-when-to-buy-your-stock.aspx.

Gad, Sham. "When To Sell Stock." *Investopedia.* Last Modified June 1, 2021.
https://www.investopedia.com/articles/stocks/10/when-to-sell-stocks.asp.

Hayes, Adam. "Mutual Funds." *Investopedia.* Last Modified October 3, 2020.
https://www.investopedia.com/terms/m/mutualfund.asp.

Hayes, Adam. "What Is an Investment?" *Investopedia.* Last modified
February 25, 2021. https://www.investopedia.com/terms/i/investment.asp.

Investopedia. "What Is the Ideal Number of Stocks To Have in a Portfolio?" Last Modified January 26, 2021. https://www.investopedia.com/ask/answers/05/optimalportfoliosize.asp.

Kagan, Julia. "Pay Yourself First." *Investopedia*. Last Modified April 25, 2021. https://www.investopedia.com/terms/p/payyourselffirst.asp.

Kennon, Joshua. "The Power of Compound Interest." *The Balance*. Last Modified June 6, 2021. https://www.thebalance.com/the-power-of-compound-interest-358054.

Kurt, Daniel. "Emergency Fund." *Investopedia*. Last Modified June 29, 2021. https://www.investopedia.com/terms/e/emergency_fund.asp.

Levitt, Aaron. "Why Should I Pay Myself First?" *Investopedia*. Last Modified September 29, 2019. https://www.investopedia.com/ask/answers/12/pay-yourself.asp.

Lioudis, Nick. '"he Importance of Diversification." *Investopedia*. Last Modified January 29, 2021. https://www.investopedia.com/investing/importance-diversification/#:~:text=Diversification%20can%20help%20an%20investor,of%20an%20asset's%20price%20movements.&text=You%20can%20reduce%20the%20risk,diversify%20among%20different%20asset%20classes.

Likos, Paulina. "How To Pick Stocks: 7 Things All Beginner Investors Should Know." *US News: Money*. September 11, 2020. https://money.usnews.com/investing/investing-101/slideshows/how-to-pick-stocks-things-all-beginner-investors-should-know.

O'Shea, Arielle. "What Is a Robo-Advisor and Is One Right for You?" *Nerd-Wallet*. March 12, 2021. https://www.nerdwallet.com/article/investing/what-is-a-robo-advisor.

Palmer, Barclay. "5 Tips For Diversifying Your Portfolio." *Investopedia*. Last Modified June 3, 2021. https://www.investopedia.com/articles/03/072303.asp.

Pant, Paula. "The Right Percentage of Income To Save Each Month." *The Balance*. Last Modified June 7, 2020. https://www.thebalance.com/how-much-money-should-you-save-each-month-453930.

Pinkasovitch, Arthur. "How To Pick A Stock: Basic Best Practices For New Investors." *Investopedia*. Last Modified May 4, 2021. https://www.investopedia.com/articles/basics/11/how-to-pick-a-stock.asp.

Porter, TJ. "What Is a Mutual Fund: Definition, Types, Pros and Cons." *Money Crashers*. March 26, 2021. https://www.moneycrashers.com/mutual-fund-types-pros-cons/.

Pritchard, Justin. "What Is Compound Interest?" *The Balance*. Last Modified May 9, 2021. https://www.thebalance.com/compound-interest-4061154.

Roberge, Eric. "A Guide To Determine How Much To Save Each Month." *Forbes*. Last Modified October 7, 2020. https://www.google.com/amp/s/www.forbes.com/sites/ericroberge/2020/10/07/a-guide-to-determine-how-much-to-save-each-month/amp/.

Royal, James. "Ally Invest Review 2021." *Bankrate*. n.d., accessed June 24, 2021. https://www.bankrate.com/investing/brokerage-reviews/ally-invest/.

Royal, James. "Best Online Brokers For Beginners in July 2021." *Bankrate*. August 1, 2021. https://www.bankrate.com/investing/best-online-brokers-for-beginners/.

Royal, James. "ETrade Review 2021." *Bankrate*. n.d., accessed June 21, 2021. https://www.bankrate.com/investing/brokerage-reviews/e-trade/.

Royal, James. "TD Ameritrade Review 2021." *Bankrate*. n.d., accessed June 21, 2021. https://www.bankrate.com/investing/brokerage-reviews/td-ameritrade/.

Royal, James. "Vanguard Review 2021." *Bankrate*. n.d., accessed June 21, 2021. https://www.bankrate.com/investing/brokerage-reviews/vanguard/.

Royal, James. "Webull Review 2021." *Bankrate*. n.d., accessed June 21, 2021. https://www.bankrate.com/investing/brokerage-reviews/webull/.

Saad, Amena. "How Many Stocks Should You Own and Why There Is No Single Right Answer." *Business Insider*. Last Modified March 1, 2021. https://www.businessinsider.com/how-many-stocks-should-i-own?r=US&IR=T.

Shashikant, Uma. "The Story of How a Retiree Started Investing at 77 and Built a Fortune for His Heirs in 12 Years." *The Economic Times*. Last Modified August 14, 2018. https://www.google.com/amp/s/m.economictimes.com/wealth/invest/the-story-of-how-a-retiree-started-investing-at-77-and-built-a-fortune-for-his-heirs-in-12-years/amp_articleshow/65364200.cms.

SoFi. "How To Know When To Buy, Hold or Sell Stock." January 5, 2021. https://www.sofi.com/learn/content/when-to-buy-stocks/?_cf_chl_jschl_tk__=63b283bbef8e1befb4cc2d97902a7d8ef656c6aa-1625306503-0-AUyFXycXtCHwACKB-RBi0BdnYoY-AmlGV1A5UrWijlpuTbAbYC64HeXoVzzOYa_pjabpy5qxXEa3qHt27-L9cCfH_vFDT9hn8VDoqAXBuQc9wTLfOIdactoHAO8uXp6SymuWrsXx9azu-NfRqWVVuCxtJ1NBFHGxaYtAcHdryQrxoyzSEFoypZ9nnRf33QqyWKZPh7ujWh8LvUVXpiSFJEY5_WEKjU1_JrYTBPfvvJlQscJbNCsGJ1fuo387atCB_FBDnXoEnttJq6PJa5bEShOMN4-AtJTYMoud2I4ty13-2bCnbjybys2Nkejc9IW_6RKLjsFgOAXU9wD8FvDT5U4SEh2RtzKqDf6GLeLDl3MkWa4lPeOG-fkYARuDRKN4BjggfCuSbxp38tRswWWg9B2Z_DrofCA9NzhcGPgIFmAnp_94Ddn67XWIPpaTp98tDYuY8ka-VMEPNoGynCAQfJLE-yz1QBtwjkrVo1v4y7HUH3UgV5orW5ncAENvqbooSA.

SoFi. "How To Know When To Sell Stock." April 26, 2021. https://www.sofi.com/learn/content/when-to-sell-a-stock/.

Stockbrokers.com. "Online Brokerage Comparison Tool." Last Modified July 3, 2021. https://www.stockbrokers.com/compare.

Tarver, Evan. "6 Investing Mistakes the Ultra Wealthy Don't Make." *Investopedia*. Last Modified June 22, 2021. https://www.investopedia.com/articles/investing/093015/6-investing-mistakes-ultra-wealthy-dont-make.asp.

TD Ameritrade. "Why Choose TD Ameritrade." [Web Page]. n.d. https://www.tdameritrade.com/why-td-ameritrade.html

Teachers Insurance Annuity Association. "The Importance of Having An Emergency Fund." n.d., accessed June 12, 2021. https://www.tiaa.org/public/offer/insights/managing-your-money/the-importance-of-having-an-emergency-fund.

The Economic Times. "Core and Satellite Portfolio Management a Popular Investment Method." Last Modified August 11, 2011. https://m.economictimes.com/wealth/personal-finance-news/core-and-satellite-portfolio-management-a-popular-investment-method/articleshow/9560863.cms?_oref=cook.

Tuovila, Alicia. "What Are Company Earnings?" *Investopedia.* Last Modified May 1, 2021. https://www.investopedia.com/terms/e/earnings.asp.

U.S. Department of Labor. "Minimum Wage." [Web Page]. n.d., accessed on June 15, 2021. https://www.dol.gov/general/topic/wages/minimumwage.

Vanguard. "Portfolio Management: Sticking With Your Plan." n.d., accessed June 21, 2021. https://investor.vanguard.com/investing/portfolio-management/.

Vanguard. "Why Investors Choose Vanguard." [Web Page]. n.d. https://investor.vanguard.com/why-vanguard.

Voigt, Kevin. "What Is an Index Fund? An Easy Way To Enter the Market." *NerdWallet.* March 19, 2021. https://www.nerdwallet.com/article/investing/what-is-an-index-fund.

Webull. "Enjoy Tech. Enjoy Investing." [Web Page]. n.d. https://www.webull.com/.

Weliver, David. "How To Invest: The Smart Way To Make Your Money Grow." Money Under 30. Last Modified August 17, 2021. https://www.moneyunder30.com/how-to-invest.